TAKING
on IRAN

UPDATED EDITION

TAKING on IRAN

Strength, Diplomacy, and the Iranian Threat

Abraham D. Sofaer

Foreword by
George P. Shultz

HOOVER INSTITUTION PRESS

STANFORD UNIVERSITY | STANFORD, CALIFORNIA

The Hoover Institution on War, Revolution and Peace, founded at Stanford University in 1919 by Herbert Hoover, who went on to become the thirty-first president of the United States, is an interdisciplinary research center for advanced study on domestic and international affairs. The views expressed in its publications are entirely those of the authors and do not necessarily reflect the views of the staff, officers, or Board of Overseers of the Hoover Institution.

www.hoover.org

Hoover Institution Press Publication No. 637

Hoover Institution at Leland Stanford Junior University, Stanford, California 94305-6010

First printing 2013
20 18 17 16 15 14 13   9 8 7 6 5 4 3 2 1

Manufactured in the United States of America

The paper used in this publication meets the minimum Requirements of the American National Standard for Information Sciences—Permanence of Paper for Printed Library Materials, ANSI/NISO Z39.48-1992. ∞

Cataloging-in-Publication Data is available from the Library of Congress.

ISBN 978-0-8179-1634-3 (cloth. : alk. paper)
ISBN 978-0-8179-1636-7 (e-book versions)

Contents

Foreword

The danger humanity faces from nuclear weapons is our most urgent diplomatic challenge. It calls for as broad an array of responses as possible to enhance the prospects of success. This book provides an alternative to war and containment in dealing with the seemingly intractable problem of Iran's nuclear threat.

The Islamic Republic of Iran seems determined—despite legal commitments to the contrary—to develop nuclear weapons along with the missiles needed to deliver them. If Iran acquires those weapons, it will feel even more confident than it does today to continue with impunity its policy of supporting surrogate and terrorist attacks on the US and our allies. A nuclear-armed Iran will set off a race for nuclear weapons by Sunni states that even now regard Shia Iran as a threat. And it will fuel the fear Iran's leaders have generated that such weapons would be used to "wipe Israel off the map." From a broader standpoint, allowing any new member to the "Nuclear Club" increases the danger of further proliferation and ultimately of nuclear war; adding Iran would be especially foolhardy.

So what should the US and its allies do to keep Iran from acquiring nuclear weapons? Wishful thinking about regime change has not worked. The UN Security Council will not adopt the necessary measures. Sanctions may bring Iran to the table if they are strong enough; but what if they are not?

The two options being debated—preventive attack and containment—both carry huge risks. Attacks on Iran's nuclear sites would be widely condemned, costly, unpopular with the Iranian people, and might well fail. Presidents Truman and Eisenhower rejected using preventive force to keep the Soviet Union from acquiring nuclear weapons for many sound reasons—not the least of which was the problem of what to do, after destroying a country's nuclear program, to keep it from starting another.

Although containment carries fewer immediate risks, it rests on the premises that Iran can be deterred and that the consequences of a nuclear-armed Iran would prove manageable. Those premises could prove mistaken, with catastrophic consequences. At some point, the US may have to choose between these two options. Until then, the US should try any sensible alternative that increases the prospect of an outcome that avoids both a major war as well as a nuclear-armed Iran.

My colleague, former State Department Legal Adviser Abraham D. Sofaer, has provided an alternative that should have been implemented long ago and that would be appropriate even if Iran had no nuclear program. He correctly points out that the Iranian Revolutionary Guard Corps (IRGC) and its Quds Force, which operate under the Grand Ayatollah, have supported and conducted attacks on US forces, allies, and interests for over thirty years. And with the single exception of US operations in the Persian Gulf in 1987–88, they have done so with impunity.

Sofaer has compiled a chilling list of IRGC actions against the US, primarily through its surrogate Hezbollah but also through its support for al-Qaeda, the Sadrists, Hamas, and now the Taliban. It includes the Marine barracks and US Embassy bombings in Lebanon, the Khobar barracks bombing in Saudi Arabia, providing weapons and active leadership to our enemies in Iraq and Afghanistan, and most recently an attempt to kill Saudi Arabia's ambassador to the US in Washington, DC. These actions and others have resulted in the deaths of at least one thousand American soldiers, and many thousands of non-combatants. Yet no US administration has used its legal right to defend the US from IRGC-sponsored attacks. The US needs to deal effectively with the *present* danger of Iranian aggression, while also addressing the *potential* danger that would be posed if Iran became a nuclear power.

Sofaer points out the key differences between implementing a preventive attack on Iran's nuclear program, on the one hand, and using defensive force to deter IRGC aggression, on the other. Preventive attacks on the nation's many nuclear facilities would be widely viewed as illegal and illegitimate, difficult and costly to implement, unpopular among the Iranian people, and likely to fail in the long run. Responding to IRGC aggression would be widely acknowledged as lawful and legitimate, easier and less costly to implement because a broader range of targets would be appropriate, and certain to be less widely opposed by Iranians, who fear and disdain the IRGC and its operations.

Frankly, I cannot understand why the US has so long endured IRGC aggression. Responding to it should be the first order of business in dealing with the Iranian threat. The IRGC has gotten away with literal murder for much too long. Iran is responsible for IRGC actions regardless of the level of political approval given by its government for each IRGC operation. We should have taken on Hezbollah and its IRGC supporters in 1983, after they killed 284 Marines. Instead, we tried to trade arms for hostages. And that pattern continued. Presidents Clinton, both Bushes, and now Obama have all failed to respond to IRGC aggression.

Most recently, President Obama, who properly brought Osama bin Laden to justice, has allowed his law enforcement officials to indict rather than hunt down those we know were planning to kill the Saudi ambassador in our national capital. How many times do we need to indict murderers who are being given sanctuary within the countries they are serving before recognizing that such remedies are ineffective? These same people used the Iranian embassy and diplomatic pouch to enable Hezbollah to destroy the Jewish community center in Buenos Aires, and arrest warrants have been outstanding for some of the perpetrators for many years. Meanwhile, Iran has given promotions to some of those charged and treated them all as heroes.

Responding to IRGC aggression is not only a right the US may lawfully exercise, but is also something we need to do for all the reasons Sofaer lays out. How Iran will react is hard to predict. The IRGC, for example, may continue to behave like the criminal organization it is. But the Iranian government is, if anything, likely to take the US more seriously, as it did after our navy's 1987 and 1988 operations in the Gulf, and after the US twice overwhelmed Saddam Hussein and pushed al-Qaeda and the Taliban out of Afghanistan. Strength appropriately exercised, rather than threats of possible future actions, will get Iran's attention and send a concrete and credible message its leaders need to hear.

The lawful use of defensive strength against the IRGC could, in addition to deterring IRGC aggression, provide important diplomatic leverage. The US has been ineffective in negotiating with Iran since 1979. An important reason for this is our lack of strength in responding to IRGC outrages, which is evident in each administration's actions related to Iran. Strength is the key to getting Iran to negotiate in earnest. But strength will not itself ensure a good outcome. The US must itself be ready to negotiate in earnest, and that requires the application of sound diplomatic practices.

Abe Sofaer led negotiations for the US with Iran in The Hague for five years. He knows how Iranian diplomats operate, and he has had the patience to work with them. He settled thousands of cases and made progress on many issues. His methodical exposition of the deficient practices the US has used in negotiating with Iran is a contribution that goes beyond the US/Iranian confrontation. His most important point is based on our experience during the Reagan Administration, when we had to decide whether to negotiate with the Soviets even when they behaved abominably. Many conservatives opposed talking to the Soviets because of their horrendous misconduct. We knew, however, that if we linked Soviet misconduct to our willingness to negotiate, we would never get to talk. It made no sense to refuse to negotiate with the Soviets when we wanted to and needed to negotiate with them. We wanted to convince the Soviets to do plenty of things that they would certainly not have done without our efforts. I explained our rationale to Congress in 1985, arguing that the proper response to Soviet misconduct was to push back against it, not to refuse to negotiate when engagement served US interests:

> Whether important negotiations ought to be interrupted after some Soviet outrage will always be a complex calculation. When the Soviets shot down the Korean Air Lines passenger plane in 1983, President Reagan made sure the world knew the full unvarnished truth about the atrocity; nevertheless, he also sent our arms control negotiators back to Geneva, because he believed that a reduction in nuclear weapons was a critical priority.
>
> In short, our "way of thinking" must seek a sustainable strategy geared to American goals and interests, in the light of Soviet behavior but not just a reaction to it. Such a strategy requires a continuing willingness to solve problems through negotiation where this serves our interests (and presumably mutual interests). Our leverage will come from creating objective realities that will give the Soviets a growing stake in better relations with us across the board: by modernizing our defenses, assisting our friends, and confronting Soviet challenges. We must learn to pursue a strategy geared to long-term thinking and based on both negotiation and strength simultaneously, if we are to build a stable U.S.-Soviet relationship for the next century.[1]

The record shows that the US has taken a different approach with Iran, and the reason is plain enough. We have been unwilling to push back against Iranian misconduct. As a result, and in an effort to seem to be doing something useful, we have refused to negotiate. Administration after administration, Republican and Democratic, has pretended that refusing to negotiate with Iran is an act reflecting strength. It is not. Refusing to talk to Iran has been a substitute for strength, rooted in the failure to act. Our failure to defend ourselves against IRGC attacks has succeeded only in convincing the IRGC it can act against the US with impunity. Our failure to talk has succeeded only in reducing the prospects for progress on the issues in US/Iranian relations that need to be addressed.

In my view, no rational case could be made for failing to defend our troops, allies, and interests against outright aggression and murder by a second-rate terrorist force. Could anyone seriously suggest that Iran appreciates US restraint in the face of such hostile conduct? When the US exercised its superior power against Iran in the Gulf in 1988, and against Saddam Hussein and the Taliban and al-Qaeda thereafter, Iran's interest in engagement with the US increased rather than declined. That the IRGC continued to support surrogate attacks and terrorism while Iran's government was seeking to engage our government was reason for us to respond to IRGC aggression directly, not to refuse to talk with those in Iran seeking to improve relations.

The situation between the US and Iran cannot be equated with what the US faced in dealing with the Soviet Union. But the policy of combining strength and diplomacy is universally valid. Both elements are necessary for success. We must not let our natural aversion to war lead us to oppose every use of force, however legitimate and essential to establish credibility; and we must not allow our natural impatience with deception and duplicity lead us to oppose every diplomatic effort, however properly prepared and promising. With regard to Iran, the US needs, first and foremost, to defend itself and its interests consistently against IRGC aggression. It then needs to respond effectively to the opportunities for engagement that are more likely to result.

This book explains how US policy can achieve both these objectives—and thereby reduce the Iranian threat without the risks of launching a preventive war or attempting to contain a nuclear-armed Iran.

GEORGE P. SHULTZ
U.S. Secretary of State 1982–87,
Distinguished Fellow
Hoover Institution
Stanford University

Acknowledgments

This book was triggered by the incongruity I experienced first-hand as a member of the Reagan Administration when we were dealing simultaneously with the threats posed by the Soviet Union and Iran. We dealt with the Soviets with intensity and professionalism. We resisted Soviet aggression and negotiated solutions. We dealt with Iran, on the other hand, in an off-handed manner, failing to defend against surrogate attacks in Lebanon and elsewhere, tolerating the seizure of US hostages, and swinging wildly in our diplomacy from a refusal to negotiate on political issues to directly appealing to Iran's leaders in the Iran/Contra Affair to release our hostages in exchange for the sale of military equipment. For years since that time I have watched the threat posed by Iran grow due to the failure of the US to apply to US/Iranian relations the toughness and realism that paid off in our dealings with the Soviet Union.

Throughout my work on this book, I have had the support and guidance of former Secretary of State George P. Shultz, the architect of US/Soviet policy under President Reagan. He encouraged me to write this book, and the insights that underlie the work are his: strength and diplomacy go together, and the refusal to negotiate is not a policy but more often an excuse for weakness.

Being at the Hoover Institution has been a great benefit, both in general and with regard to each of the scholarly projects I have been involved with over a period of 18 years. I appreciate the support I have had from John Raisian, our director, from several of my colleagues, and from the yearly crop of National Security Fellows, who have taken an interest in all my national security projects and contributed to them based on the invaluable insights they have gained—as soldiers and diplomats—through their service to country. I appreciate in particular the guidance provided by Lieutenant Commander Manuel Hernandez with regard to the rules applicable to navy commanders in the Persian Gulf. I am also grateful to my wife, Marian Scheuer Sofaer, for many improvements to the draft.

Among the other people who have contributed to my understanding of the issues are Michael Armacost, who has served the US in many important offices, including Under Secretary of State for Political and Military Affairs during my tenure as Legal Adviser; Dr. Abbas Malekzadeh Milani, Hoover's resident expert on Iran and Director of Iranian Studies at Stanford, who read the rough draft and provided invaluable feedback; Dr. Sidney Drell; Admiral Gary Roughead, former Chief of Naval Operations and current resident scholar at Hoover; former Secretary of Defense William Perry; and my ever-helpful colleague, Thomas Henriksen. My friend, and Hoover Overseer, Marc Abramowitz also provided helpful comments and suggestions on the draft.

Many research assistants worked hard over a period of several years, for the short periods of time they were available, to document the facts on which I have relied. They include: Leisel Bogan, Tom Church, Lakshmi Eassey, Janis Hall, Rachel Hildebrandt, Isaac Kardon, Nathan R. Lazarus, Terry Long, Courtney Matteson, Joshua G. Nimer, Megan Reiss, Brian Vo, Jay Weil, and Cheryl Hedges, who provided invaluable assistance as research coordinator during several months of the work.

Thanks are also due to the Hoover Press and to Shana Farley and Chris Dauer in Hoover's Marketing and Communications Department for helping me publish this book initially on the Internet. The current, print edition adds new material and some revisions. The Hoover Press provided an excellent editor, Roger Williams, who helped clean up errors of style and expression. Finally, neither this project nor any other I have been involved with could have been completed without the dedicated and intelligent help of my executive assistant, Grace Goldberger.

TAKING
on IRAN

Introduction

The threat posed by Iran to international peace and security is approaching a crisis. After compiling a thirty-year record as the world's most active state supporter of terrorism—led by its Pasadran, or Revolutionary Guard Corps (IRGC)—Iran seems determined to develop nuclear weapons. Its aims are not merely defensive or solely based on national pride. The nation's rulers do seek to preserve their religious system, but they are also attempting to lead an Islamic resurgence in which Western powers would be driven from all Islamic countries. In pursuing these objectives Iran has intervened in the affairs of many states. It has also attacked and threatened the US and other states that interfere with its aspirations. And it calls repeatedly for wiping Israel off the face of the Earth while providing weapons to Israel's enemies to advance that end.

The US has used force against Iran only once since the 1979 Islamic Revolution: during 1987 and 1988, after Iran attacked US-flagged vessels and mined the Persian Gulf. Otherwise, the US has tried dealing with the Iranian threat and its nuclear program through hoped for "regime change," diplomatic isolation, and economic sanctions combined with threats, negotiations, and outright appeals (described in Chapter 1). All these efforts have failed to convince Iran to curb its nuclear program or to stop supporting surrogate attacks and terrorism.

Iran's illegal support of attacks against the US has been extensive and brutal. These activities (described in Chapter 2) started in Lebanon with the creation of Hezbollah, the bombing of the US Embassy and Marine barracks, and the taking of US nationals there as hostages. They have continued to the present in the form of lethal assistance to Sadrists in Iraq and the Taliban in Afghanistan, and with the attempted assassination of Saudi Arabia's ambassador on US soil. The effort is led by the IRGC, which together with its Quds and Basij forces, have been responsible for protecting the Islamic character of the state. The IRGC controls essential military capacities (including Iran's nuclear and missile programs) and foreign operations, and it is charged with enforcing Islamic principles on the people. Its influence has increased greatly in recent years. IRGC members and former members participate in Iran's regular government (through legislative, ministerial, and judicial positions), and the organization has accumulated great wealth and economic influence through its control of smuggling in the Gulf and the state contracts it obtains for IRGC-controlled construction firms and other entities.

Despite this extensive history of IRGC support for attacks on the US, the latter has focused virtually exclusively on Iran's nuclear program in attempting to deal with the Iranian threat. The nuclear program has nevertheless progressed. US experts believe that Iran already has the capability to make nuclear weapons, though the speed and efficiency with which that could be done is vigorously debated. (Estimates of the time required range from several months to several years.)

Many world leaders have declared that Iran must not be permitted to develop nuclear weapons. But keeping Iran from developing nuclear weapons will take more than determination and rhetoric; it will be difficult and costly to achieve, if not impossible. Increased pressure is being exerted on Iran through a variety of sanctions. But the effects of these measures have varied and have been disrupted or dissipated by Iranian actions. The measures have as yet failed to translate into any progress in the negotiations between Iran and the

"P5+1" powers (consisting of the Permanent Members of the United Nations Security Council (UNSC) (Britain, China, France, Russia, and the US), together with Germany).[1] President Mahmoud Ahmadinejad has reiterated that Iran "will not retreat" from its nuclear "rights" despite UNSC resolutions ordering Iran to stop enrichment and all missile-development programs.[2]

The US continues to hope that economic sanctions will force Iran to accept limits on its nuclear program sufficient to constrain its operation to peaceful purposes. But what if Iran is unwilling to accept such limits? The distinct possibility exists that the P5+1 negotiations, like all before them, will fail. Yet only two alternatives to a negotiated settlement are being widely discussed: launching military attacks on Iran's nuclear program; or accepting a nuclear-armed Iran and attempting to contain it. As virtually all analysts and commentators recognize, both these options present grave risks, described below.

An alternative, viable approach exists by which the US could successfully deal with Iran's nuclear program without resorting either to preventive attacks or accepting nuclear arms. Specifically, the US could exercise its right to defend its forces, nationals, and interests from IRGC aggression. For over thirty years (as described in Chapter 3), US administrations have failed to use force to defend against IRGC-supported attacks, relying instead on sanctions, threats, and diplomatic approaches that have shifted wildly from refusing to negotiate with Iran to appealing to Iranian leaders for a better relationship. Defending against IRGC aggression would give the US strategic flexibility, enabling it to increase the pressure on Iran with measures short of preventive military attacks aimed at destroying its nuclear program.

Defending against Iranian-sponsored attacks and terrorism is a long-overdue, practical, and principled strategic imperative that would be necessary even if Iran obtained nuclear weapons, just as resistance to conventional Soviet threats was necessary after the Soviets acquired them. The US has long needed to send a clear message to the IRGC and its supporters in the Iranian government that its illegal conduct will no longer be tolerated.

Military actions against IRGC targets related to its surrogate or terrorist attacks on the US would (as explained in Chapter 4) be legally defensible, legitimate, practical, and likely to succeed. Exercising self-defense against IRGC aggression is also essential to restore US credibility, and the available evidence indicates that a firm response to IRGC aggression is likely to convince Iran to reduce its unlawful activities and increase its interest in negotiating. Instead of responding directly to each form of IRGC misconduct, US administrations have responded by refusing to negotiate or by imposing sanctions, remedies that have produced neither deterrence nor diplomatic progress. Ending IRGC impunity would increase the potential utility of negotiations.

If Iran responds to US defensive actions by seeking genuine diplomatic engagement, as it has in the past, the US should make clear in advance that it is prepared to apply a set of diplomatic practices very different from those it has thus far utilized in dealing with Iran. The US should engage Iran on the basis of the practices applied in US/Soviet negotiations (described in Chapter 5), specifically: rhetorical restraint; regime engagement; limited linkage; a broad agenda; and forum flexibility.

In sum, taking on Iran cannot safely be restricted to a strategy based on economic sanctions and ineffective diplomacy. The risk that current US policy will fail is too great, and the consequences too serious, to rely on the current policy as the exclusive means of dealing with threats from Iran short of attacking its nuclear program. Instead, the US should exercise its right to respond to IRGC aggression, thereby increasing the likelihood that Iran will negotiate in earnest, and enabling the US in turn to engage in the disciplined manner required for success. Effective diplomacy based on strength is the most likely formula for avoiding the highly undesirable options of attacking Iran's nuclear program or attempting to contain its actions as a nuclear-armed state.

CHAPTER 1

Dealing with the Iranian Threat

The Islamic Republic of Iran has posed a threat to international peace and security since 1979. The range of Iranian misconduct has been broad, including the seizure of US diplomats as hostages, suppression of the rights and liberties of Iranian nationals, assassinating the Islamic regime's enemies in foreign countries, supporting Shia groups against Sunni-controlled governments, arming terrorist groups (including Sunnis) that have attacked US soldiers in Lebanon, Iraq, and Afghanistan, and abetting terrorist attacks in many other countries, notably Israel. The US has repeatedly protested these activities and has issued numerous threats to counteract them; but it has done little or nothing to deter them, concentrating its efforts instead on Iran's nuclear program.

The official US position, fully supported in principle by several other leaders, is that, because a nuclear-armed Iran would threaten international peace and security, it is "unacceptable." US President Barack Obama has promised to "prevent" Iran from obtaining nuclear weapons.[1] French President Nicolas Sarkozy insisted that the program end, and he proposed the current effort to have Europe ban the import of Iranian oil and block Iran from banking transactions.[2] German Chancellor Angela Merkel has said, "It is a must to prevent Iran from having nuclear weapons."[3] Prime Minister Benjamin

Netanyahu of Israel has promised to prevent a state committed to Israel's destruction from acquiring the means for bringing it about.[4]

US statements have become increasingly specific. Secretary of Defense Leon Panetta said, for example, on December 19, 2011, that Iran could develop a nuclear weapon during 2012 and "That's a red line for us and, . . . obviously, for the Israelis. If they proceed . . . with developing a nuclear weapon then we will take whatever steps necessary to stop it."[5] When asked, "Including military steps?" he replied in language that has become formulaic: "There are no options off the table."[6] President Obama said in his 2012 State of the Union address that he was determined to "prevent" a nuclear-armed Iran, thereby suggesting a willingness to disregard the conventional, international law prerequisite for the use of self-defense—an attack or threat of imminent attack:

> Let there be no doubt: America is determined to prevent Iran from getting a nuclear weapon, and I will take no options off the table to achieve that goal. But a peaceful resolution of this issue is still possible, and far better, and if Iran changes course and meets its obligations, it can rejoin the community of nations.[7]

President Obama and Secretary Panetta are undoubtedly sincere in their desire to keep Iran from obtaining nuclear weapons. Yet the statements they and other Obama Administration officials have made in describing US intentions resemble those made by officials in former US administrations expressing their determination to prevent North Korea's development of nuclear weapons. President Clinton said in 1993, for example, that "North Korea cannot be allowed to develop a nuclear bomb . . . [W]e have to be very firm about it."[8] And on October 4, 2006, Assistant Secretary Christopher Hill, US negotiator with North Korea under President George W. Bush, declared that "we are not going to live with a nuclear North Korea" and that North Korea "can have a future or it can have these weapons. It cannot have both."[9] The measures actually implemented by the US to prevent what presidents and high-level officials characterized as "unacceptable" failed to stop North Korea from obtaining nuclear weapons and have thus far failed to stop Iran from pursuing the capacities it needs to achieve the same objective.

In attempting to curb Iran's nuclear aspirations, the US has shifted among several approaches, including regime change, sanctions, negotiations ("engagement"), and direct appeals. Each approach—alone or in combination—has failed thus far to convince Iran to modify its nuclear program in a manner that negates an intention to develop nuclear weapons.

Regime Change

Since the Islamic regime took power in 1979, many political leaders, officials, and experts have advanced the notion that Iran's threat to international peace and security could and should be eliminated through regime change brought on by sanctions, political isolation, covert operations, and internal pressure. Thirty years of Islamic rule have undermined the credibility of this strategy, at least in the absence of far more intrusive methods than have been or are likely to be authorized. The notion of regime change as the solution to the Iranian nuclear threat continues to emerge, however, in one form or another, creating unrealistic expectations and undermining any possibility of successful engagement.[10] While the US has insisted that regime change is not its official policy, this means in practice that the US takes no action within Iran to bring about regime change, which would amount to an illegal intervention. US policy has continued to rely on regime change from within. As Henry Kissinger has testified: "The current US policy of refusing to engage Iran was founded on the belief that the regime would collapse from within," an assumption he noted may be incorrect.[11]

Calls for displacing the Islamic regime invariably lack any feasible plan of action.[12] A petition drawn up in 1989 and signed by 186 members of Congress, advocated that the US government support the "opposition" rather than try to help the moderate regime then in power. Had President Akbar Rafsanjani been removed at that time, however, he would have been unable to secure the release of the US hostages being held in Lebanon.[13] Congress thereafter passed legislation providing $18 million for efforts in Iran to help Iranian "civil society" and pro-democracy groups.[14] The strategy backfired. Reformers in Iran dared not apply for this money. The Iranian government, meanwhile, cited the bill as a basis for intensifying its repression and responded to the legislation by providing roughly the same amount to undermine US attacks on Islam. This legislation was soon followed by IRGC assistance to Saudi Hezbollah in its attack on the Khobar Towers.

The US should actively support a "freedom" agenda for the Iranian people, just as it actively supported freedom within the former Soviet Union.[15] But the public demonstrations that have taken place within Iran have thus far been aimed at economic issues and corruption, and the government has brutally suppressed them. It is unclear whether most Iranians favor overturning the Islamic regime.[16] Disorder would have to become widespread, and be more broadly aimed, in order to pose a significant threat to the regime. Some US officials appear to have believed, and some may still believe, that the regime "is discredited, a house of cards ready to be pushed over the precipice," but that conclusion is speculative at best.[17] Predictions of regime change in North Korea, by a panel of government and outside experts convened by the CIA in 1997,[18] may have contributed to the failure of US efforts to keep that regime from becoming a nuclear power.[19]

Advocates of regime change share a common assumption, rejected by many national security experts, that it provides a more effective way to reduce the Iranian threat than preventing nuclear proliferation. Robert Kagan has written, for example: "Were Iran ruled by a democratic government, even an imperfect one, we would be much less concerned about its weaponry." Kagan's observation is obviously correct but hardly proof that regime change is a workable strategy. Such arguments lend support, moreover, to Ahmadinejad's "claims that it is the [Islamic] regime, not its nuclear program, that the United States finds objectionable."[20] Henry Kissinger, by contrast, has written: "Focusing on regime change as the road to denuclearization confuses the issue. The United States should oppose nuclear weapons in North Korea and Iran regardless of the government that builds them."[21] In fact, regime change is unlikely to result in new leaders who favor giving up enrichment and other troubling aspects of Iran's nuclear program.

In any event, efforts to bring about regime change are no substitute for acting to deter IRGC aggression. Defending against IRGC actions might be helpful, in fact, in bringing about a regime change that reduces the threat posed by Iran. If Iran is held accountable for irresponsible IRGC conduct, that organization may lose some of the political and economic power it has been able to acquire. Currently, as Scott Sagan has written, it is "misguided simply to hope that eventual regime change in Tehran would end the nuclear danger." There is "no reason to assume that, even if they wanted to, central political authorities in Tehran could completely control the details of nuclear operations by the Islamic Revolutionary Guard Corps"; a new regime would be preferable only if it were both inclined and able to curb IRGC aims and operations.[22]

Sanctions

Economic sanctions have a long, unsuccessful history in US dealings with Iran. In large part, this is because the most severe types of sanctions imposed have had little support from other states, including US allies. Germany, Japan, and Russia are among the states that have grasped the economic opportunities that the US has given up in its effort to create pressure on Iran to curb its nuclear program. President George W. Bush acknowledged in January 2005: "We're relying upon others, because we've sanctioned ourselves out of influence with Iran."[23] In the last several years, as a result of the US decision to join the Europeans in offering engagement and benefits to Iran, the other permanent members of the Security Council and Germany have agreed to join the US in adopting resolutions prohibiting enrichment and ballistic missile development, and imposing several rounds of sanctions. Iran has disregarded the resolutions,[24] even though the sanctions have had significant, adverse effects on its economy.

Further escalation in sanctions took place after November 2011, when French President Sarkozy proposed that the European Union (EU) member states, together with the US, Canada, Japan, and others, stop purchasing Iranian oil. Many states have agreed to this embargo, and the US and other supporters are attempting to convince as many purchasers of Iranian oil as possible that they should join. Saudi Arabia has agreed to supply oil to any state that needs it to replace what otherwise would have been bought from Iran. Maritime insurance coverage for shipments of Iranian oil has become difficult to obtain.[25] On January 23, 2012, the EU agreed to freeze "assets of the Iranian central bank within the EU" as well as to prohibit "trade in gold, precious metals, and diamonds with Iranian public bodies."[26] On February 6, 2012, President Obama signed an executive order blocking all "property and interests in property" of the Government of Iran, the Central Bank of Iran, and Iranian financial institutions.[27] Iran has also been denied access to the SWIFT system for international financial transfers, severely limiting the nation's ability to engage in major financial transactions.[28]

The escalation of sanctions against Iran, which continues, has adversely affected its economy, but for how long and with what consequences is uncertain. Prior sanctions aimed at Iran have met with much resistance from EU states,[29] and major purchasers of Iranian oil, including China and India, have refused to accept the embargo.[30] (China reduced purchases of Iranian oil, but this may have been for the purpose of obtaining lower prices.[31]) Although

Japan and South Korea have restricted their purchases of Iranian oil, this policy may not be sustainable, because it could force them to buy expensive liquid natural gas from other states, including the US.[32] The six-month delay in implementing the oil embargo was to enable participating states to make alternative arrangements; that time also allowed Iran to make arrangements to reduce the embargo's effects.[33]

Iran is attempting to establish methods for completing financial transactions that do not depend on SWIFT and other mechanisms that are being blocked.[34] British insurers were prepared to deny coverage to tankers shipping Iranian oil, but were forced with EU support to secure a six-month delay in implementing that policy; Japan made alternative arrangements, and both China and India are likely to do so as well.[35] Iran has re-registered its merchant vessels and oil tankers in a variety of other states, increasing the difficulty of denying access. Much has been made in the press of the drastic reduction in the value of the Iranian *rial*. But many Iranians attribute this development largely to mismanagement of the national economy and faulty currency restrictions, not solely or even primarily to the sanctions; even the decline in the *rial's* value may have a positive effect on Iran's economy by making its exports cheaper.

US domestic financial sanctions on Iran have never been more comprehensive, but their effect is often exaggerated.[36] Kenneth Katzman's comprehensive study of the sanctions, for the Congressional Research Service (CRS), cites National Security Adviser Tom Donilon's statement that sanctions "coupled with mistakes and difficulties in Iran, . . . have slowed Iran's nuclear efforts," but then notes that the US Defense Department and others have concluded that sanctions have not stopped Iran's conventional and missile activities and that Iran's nuclear stockpile has continued to expand.[37] Realizing these limitations, a distinguished group of national security experts has recommended that Iran be completely isolated from access to international business; that strategy would have a powerful effect, as comprehensive sanctions did on Libya, but no realistic prospect of the adoption of "total" sanctions on Iran by the UNSC currently exists.[38]

Some analysts continue to believe (or hope) that economic sanctions will cause Iran to agree to curb its nuclear program.[39] Given the exceptions that already exist, however, plus the evasions Iran is able to develop with help from others, enhanced sanctions are unlikely to lead Iran to negotiate in earnest.[40] As Scott Sagan notes: "Washington learned with India and Pakistan in the 1980s and 1990s [that] sanctions only increase the costs of going nuclear; they do not reduce the ability of a determined government to get the bomb."[41] Foreign Minister Ali Akbar Salehi reacted to the recent escalation of sanctions by stating that "Iran, with divine assistance, has always been ready to counter such hostile actions, and we are not concerned at all about the sanctions."[42] Of course, Iran *is* concerned about the sanctions, but it demonstrated during its war with Iraq the capacity to bear economic hardship to maintain policies on which the Iranian public and its government are aligned. The adverse impact of the sanctions may in fact lead Iran to speed up rather than suspend its nuclear effort,[43] hoping that sanctions may be lifted once they have failed, as they were after Pakistan and India achieved nuclear-weapons status.

Finally, continued application or escalation of economic sanctions on Iran will receive increasing scrutiny by those concerned with their harmful impact on the population. The US government continues to casually dismiss this consideration, as it did prior to the invasion of Iraq, where sanctions did grievous harm but nonetheless failed to cause Saddam Hussein to capitulate to Security Council demands. But the fact is that, while sanctions may well fail to secure their political objectives, they are imposing significant and increasing hardship on the Iranian people. UN Secretary-General Ban Ki-moon, for example, criticized the US and EU for imposing sanctions that are injuring the well-being of innocent Iranians, increasing unemployment and shortages of food and medicines (despite exceptions for the latter that fail to be effectively applied).[44] Shirin Ebadi, a Nobel Prize winner and human rights lawyer who opposes the current Iranian regime and any nuclear weapons program, supports "targeted sanctions that weaken the government" but urges that "any sanctions that are detrimental to the people should be avoided."[45]

Negotiations and Direct Appeals

Every US administration since 1979 has at times threatened and refused to negotiate with Iran. Every administration since 1979 has also at times agreed to negotiate with Iran, sometimes with demanding preconditions, sometimes with no preconditions at all. Recently, the US has limited its interest in negotiations with Iran to demanding concessions related to its nuclear program. The P5+1 talks have included discussion of political and economic benefits, but only as incentives that would be granted for Iran's concessions on the nuclear issues. All efforts to convince Iran significantly to modify its nuclear program have failed, and Iran has repeatedly and deliberately used the negotiations, including the P5+1 talks, to deflect or delay international pressure.[46]

Several administrations have also made direct appeals to Iran for a better relationship, at times accompanied by apologies and unilateral concessions. These direct appeals, especially those associated with the Iran/Contra Affair, not only failed, but also embarrassed the US.

This failure of the US to deal successfully with the Iranian nuclear threat through diplomacy has led to a virtual avalanche of books, articles, and speeches by political leaders, former government officials, and a variety of experts concluding that negotiating with Iran would be fruitless. It is true that "engagement" with Iran on its nuclear program has failed to accomplish anything meaningful. Not all negotiations with Iran since 1979 have been fruitless, however.

Iran has remained a member of the Non-Proliferation Treaty (NPT) regime, and has allowed inspections that have been meaningful enough to enable inspectors to discover improper or questionable behavior, leading Iran at one point to sign the Additional Protocol. Iran's nuclear capacities are reasonably well known as a result of its agreement to inspections and intelligence gathering. Iran has also reached significant agreements with the US in areas other than its nuclear program, including the Algiers Accords and settlements of commercial claims in The Hague. Iran has properly implemented its settlements with the US and US nationals, as well as adverse decisions of the Iran/US Tribunal; and it has maintained the required balances in the Security Account established at the Tribunal to assure payments. It also negotiated constructively on issues related to Afghanistan and Iraq.

Moreover, the failure to secure changes in Iran's nuclear policies through negotiations may well be attributable to the failure of the US and the international community to hold the IRGC accountable for its surrogate and terrorist attacks. As several analysts have observed, Iran is a radical regime, with a revolutionary, faith-based agenda that its leadership does not want to compromise.[47] It should not be surprising that negotiations with such a regime have failed when nothing has been done to change IRGC behavior during its over thirty years of aggression.

Thus, while former Israeli Ambassador to the UN, Dore Gold, can fairly say that "Engagement has been tried in the past and doesn't work," he is also accurate in saying, "If the West tries diplomatic engagement again with the Islamic Republic, it would have to be formulated differently."[48] As he at one point suggests: "engagement and military power might work hand-in-glove for negotiating with Iran."[49]

Negotiations can be useful even with an enemy. They became fruitful in dealing with the Soviet Union, once the US responded firmly to Soviet armed interventions and other forms of aggressive behavior. In the one context in which the US defended against IRGC attacks, in the Gulf in 1987 and 1988, Iran stopped its aggressive actions, and after major US military actions against Iran's neighbors in Iraq and Afghanistan it affirmatively sought negotiations with the US. Negotiations conducted in the context of effective US responses to IRGC aggression would differ significantly from prior forms of engagement with Iran, and could well lead to useful results.

Preventive Attack or Containment?

The failure of prior efforts to deal effectively with the threat posed by Iran's nuclear program has led to an intense debate over what should be done if the P5+1 process fails, despite enhanced sanctions. Thus far, the debate over which policy to implement at that point has been between those who believe that Iran must be prevented from acquiring nuclear weapons, by force if necessary, and those who oppose a preventive attack and instead support efforts to "contain" a nuclear-armed Iran by using the means available to the US for that purpose. In this regard, the recent RAND report, *Coping with a Nuclearizing Iran*, includes—in addition to sanctions—"deterrence by denial" (for example, missile defense systems), and "deterrence by punishment" (for example, devastating retaliatory strikes), but does not mention the potential of deterrence by the exercise of self-defense.[50] A report by The Iran Project, published by the Wilson Center, on the benefits and costs of "military action," discusses only the possible effects of full-scale attacks on Iran's nuclear program, with no analysis of "military action" as a component of self-defense.[51]

Those determined to prevent Iran from acquiring nuclear weapons regard containment as unacceptable. Thirty-two U.S. Senators introduced a Sense of the Senate resolution on February 16, 2011, rejecting "any policy that would rely on containment as an option in response to the Iranian nuclear threat."[52] President Obama has said that he does "not have a policy of containment,"[53] and that the US will "prevent" Iran from obtaining nuclear weapons, suggesting that he would use force in Iran if multilateral sanctions and negotiations fail to result in a peaceful solution to the problem.

Prime Minister Netanyahu and other high-ranking Israeli officials regard a nuclear-armed Iran as an existential threat to Israel. Iran's missiles can reach Israel, its IRGC has armed Israel's enemies, and its calls for Israel's elimination as a Jewish state are profoundly disturbing.[54] The Supreme Ayatolah Khomeini gave these virtual calls for genocide their start by urging that Israel be "wiped off the map," a formulation not only repeated by current leaders, but also supplemented with even more explicitly genocidal aims. Supreme Ayatollah Khamenei has called Israel a "cancerous tumor that should be cut and will be cut." Iran's military Chief of Staff, Major Gen. Hassan Firouzabadi, has said that Iran stands for "the full annihilation of Israel."[55] President Ahmadenijad's recent formulation is that Israel's "existence" is "an insult to humanity." Given these views, some Iranian leaders may not be deterred by the possibility of even a nuclear response to an Iranian or Iranian-sponsored nuclear attack. President Ahmadinejad has indicated, for example, that he believes chaos could signal the return of the lost Mahdi.[56] Netanyahu said in a speech to the American Israel Public Affairs Committee (AIPAC) in Washington, DC, on March 5, 2012: "Israel has exactly the same policy [as President Obama]. We are determined to prevent Iran from developing nuclear weapons; we leave all options on the table; and containment is definitely not an option. The Jewish state will not allow those who seek our destruction to possess the means to achieve that goal. A nuclear-armed Iran must be stopped."[57]

An Iran with nuclear capability is also seen as a threat to other states in the region. Emir Sa'ud al-Feisal, Saudi Arabia's foreign minister, said that "Iran's involvement in the internal affairs of the nations of the region, as well as its nuclear crisis and attempts to develop its nuclear program—that will allow it to have nuclear weapons—are a clear threat to the entire region."[58] If Iran acquires nuclear weapons, Egypt, Saudi Arabia, Turkey, and perhaps other states will feel compelled to obtain them, too, to counter the increased threat these states would face. The difficulty of maintaining stability and peace in a region in which several states with conflicting ideologies and ambitions possess nuclear weapons would be vastly greater than the difficulties faced by the Soviet Union and the US in maintaining stability in a bipolar standoff.[59] In addition, it is not clear that a nuclear device given to a terrorist group could be traced to its source, a fact that reduces the deterrent value of retaliation.[60]

Advocates of a preventive attack acknowledge that it would entail significant costs and risks and that a single attack might fail or might only delay Iran's program. They view a nuclear-armed Iran as a greater risk, however, than the risks associated with preventive attack.[61] Israeli Defense Minister Ehud Barak said on April 30, 2012, for example, "Dealing with a nuclearized Iran will be far more complex, far more dangerous, and far more costly in blood and money than stopping it today. In other words, those who say 'later' may find that later is too late."[62] Some who favor an attack contend, moreover, that the cost, difficulty, and risks of a preventive attack have been exaggerated, noting that the legality and legitimacy of attacking Iran's nuclear program are strengthened by the nation's established record of supporting attacks on the US (and Israel) and of irrational behavior.[63] They argue that only two of Iran's facilities (its enrichment operations at Natanz and Fordow) are essential to its program and that they can be successfully attacked in a limited but effective air and missile bombardment, with so-called bunker-buster bombs and penetrating explosives serving as the primary weapons.[64] They regard any collateral damage as acceptable in light of the physical and strategic damage a nuclear-armed Iran could cause. They acknowledge that Iran might resume work on developing a nuclear arsenal even after a successful attack, but they would be satisfied to significantly delay development, and they feel that additional attacks should be undertaken if required.[65]

The case for a preventive attack is, for writer/commentator Norman Podhoretz, rooted in what he sees as "World War IV," a contest between freedom and "Islamofacism, yet another mutation of the totalitarian disease we defeated first in the shape of Nazism and fascism and then in the shape of Communism . . . ," and in the premise that "if Iran is to be prevented from developing a nuclear arsenal, there is no alternative to the actual use of military force—any more than there was an alternative to force if Hitler was to be stopped in 1938."[66]

Henry Kissinger has sounded a similar alarm: "If Iran acquires nuclear weapons, we will live in a new world. That is the fundamental issue we must face. And our only choice is to prevent it, or to pay the price of not having prevented it. . . . [T]his is not a tactical issue. This is a fundamental issue of a historical turn."[67] In other words, either decision, to prevent or to allow Iran to develop nuclear weapons, will have dramatic and likely irreversible consequences.

It is uncertain whether, despite their threats, President Obama and/or Israeli leaders would actually launch preventive attacks on Iran's nuclear program if they fail to convince Iran to implement acceptable limits.[68] However sincere they may be in asserting that a nuclear-armed Iran is "unacceptable," these leaders are hoping that their tough talk, together with enhanced sanctions, will lead Iran to make a deal that obviates the need to use force.[69] Their threats could, in fact, succeed in convincing Iran to negotiate an acceptable compromise. But threats and sanctions, however emphatic and damaging, will not reduce the difficulty and costs of preventive attacks. If the threats and sanctions do not work, the decision to act militarily against Iran's nuclear program, or to refrain from doing so, will have to be made on the basis of the costs and benefits perceived at that time.

US presidents and other officials emphatically asserted in years past that a nuclear-armed North Korea was "unacceptable," and its economy and people suffered greatly on account of its nuclear policy. But whether to use force to attempt to prevent North Korea from obtaining a nuclear weapon remained no less difficult a dilemma after the US had issued threats and the international community had imposed sanctions than it had been before. More than once, North Korea agreed or seemed to agree to important concessions, but these agreements were all reversed.[70] North Korea's nuclear facilities could have been destroyed from the air, but its ability to attack South Korea with massive artillery bombardments remained and could have caused millions of casualties.[71] China strongly opposed any attack on North Korea, moreover, and might have intervened on North Korea's side. US officials also realized that destroying North Korea's nuclear program provided no assurance that it would not be reconstituted and made less vulnerable to future attack.

Preventive war made no sense to President Harry Truman, morally or politically. He wrote in his memoir: "[T]here is nothing more foolish than to think that war can be stopped by war. You don't 'prevent' anything by war except peace."[72] The Truman Administration considered but eventually renounced preventive war against the Soviet Union, opting instead for a rapid build-up of US economic and military strength. National Security Council (NSC) Report 68 concluded: "A powerful blow could be delivered upon the Soviet Union, but it is estimated that these operations alone would not force or induce the Kremlin to capitulate and that the Kremlin would still be able to use the forces under its control to dominate most or all of Eurasia."[73]

President Dwight Eisenhower agreed that preventive war against the Soviet Union "ought to be considered," telling Secretary of State John Foster Dulles in 1953 that in some circumstances "we would be forced to consider whether or not our duty to future generations did not require us to initiate war at the most propitious moment that we could designate."[74] Ultimately, however, Eisenhower, too, rejected the idea, concluding that even if the US won a general, preventive war, the resources needed to maintain control and the problems that would arise during the postwar period would be beyond America's capabilities.[75] In 1954, he signed NSC-5440, which stated: "The United States and its allies must reject the concept of preventive war or acts intended to provoke war."[76] Proposals to bomb China to prevent it from developing nuclear weapons were rejected by US leaders for similar reasons. In his analysis of US policy on this subject, Jeffrey Record states: "President Johnson was simply not prepared to risk a potentially open-ended war with China for the sake of military action that would at best postpone—not prevent—China's eventual acquisition [of nuclear weapons]."[77]

These decisions not to use force preventively against the Soviet Union and China are now regarded as sound; they avoided needless, and potentially nuclear, conflicts. They are part of the policy background that has led many, if not most, US national security officials and strategic planners to decide against using force for the sole purpose of preventing a state from acquiring nuclear weapons. While US leaders have repeatedly stated that "all options" including force are "on the table" to prevent Iran from acquiring nuclear weapons, they have also recognized that preventive attacks on Iran's nuclear program would be difficult to justify, costly, and dangerous, and might well fail to achieve their ultimate purpose. Iran's program poses a far greater challenge than the single-facility programs bombed by Israel in Iraq (1981) and Syria (2007). Iran has many well-defended facilities; the most important of them, the Fordor reprocessing plant, is located inside a mountain and may be impossible to destroy from the air.[78] Moreover, some of its nuclear facilities are close to populated areas, and attacks on them might result in the emission of radioactive materials.[79]

A particularly important consideration in this regard is the proposition that, as my colleague Kori Schake wrote in 2007, Iran already has the technical abilities to make a nuclear bomb and "could likely achieve it without detection."[80] This position (though inconsistent with the stated views of some officials) has been forcefully articulated in a detailed report by Anthony H. Cordesman, which reached the following conclusions:

Iran has moved far beyond the point where it lacked the technology base to produce nuclear weapons. . . . Iran has pursued every major area of nuclear weapons development, has carried out programs that have already given it every component of a weapon except fissile material, and there is strong evidence that it has carried out programs to integrate a nuclear warhead on to its missiles. . . . Iran's efforts are part of a far broader range of efforts that have already brought it to the point where it can pursue nuclear weapons development through a range of compartmented and easily concealable programs without a formal weapons program, and even if it suspends enrichment activity.[81]

These conclusions, based on detailed findings of the International Atomic Energy Agency (IAEA), reduce to relative insignificance debates about particular negotiating positions, since virtually any continuing nuclear program would enable Iran to build a bomb if it chose to do so.[82] It no longer makes much difference, for example, whether Iran allows access to a particular site or makes efforts to clean it up in advance.[83] Even a successful attack on Iran's most vital nuclear-related sites will at most delay its program, since it is impossible to reverse the knowledge and capacities Iranian scientists have acquired; Iran will be able to reconstitute a program that is not subject to inspection, dispersed, and hidden from view.[84]

Then, too, preventive attacks pose a moral challenge in that, even though motivated by the desire to avoid human harm, they will appear to be "unprovoked" (as the RAND report says) and would therefore enable Iran to appear the victim, rather than the cause, of the resulting conflict. At that point, Iran would be widely viewed as justified in proceeding to develop nuclear weapons secretly—and in defending itself against what would widely be regarded as an illegal and illegitimate attack. The Iran Project report predicts that a preventive attack launched before clear evidence exists of Iran's intent to build a nuclear weapon would undermine the current international consensus against the regime's nuclear weapons–related activities.

These factors explain why most US officials and national security experts oppose preventive attacks on Iran, at least until it has demonstrated that it is determined to develop nuclear weapons.[85] Former Secretary of Defense William Gates said in April 2009, for example, that a strike on Iran's nuclear facilities could unify Iran and strengthen its determination to obtain nuclear weapons and that Iran's development of nuclear weapons could be prevented only if "Iranians themselves decide it's too costly."[86] Gates also discouraged an Israeli attack: "We are prepared to do what is necessary. But at this point we continue to believe that the political, economic approach that we are taking is in fact having an impact in Iran."[87] Secretary Panetta has commented that an Israeli attack might provoke Iran to respond, not only against Israel, but against the US as well.[88]

Many US officials and experts believe that Iran can successfully be deterred from using nuclear weapons through a combination of military and economic pressures,[89] missile defense (well under way),[90] and the implicit threat of massive retaliation.[91] Fareed Zakaria has denounced the notion that failing to attack Iran before it acquires nuclear weapons would be a lost opportunity: "Nations have often believed that they face a closing window to act, and almost always such thinking has led to disaster." He quotes Gideon Rose's comment on the US/UK decision not to resort to preventive attacks on the Soviet Union: "Israel is finally confronting the sort of choices the United States and Great Britain confronted more than six decades ago. Hopefully it, too, will come to recognize that absolute security is impossible to achieve in the nuclear age, and that if its enemies' nuclear programs cannot be delayed or disrupted, deterrence is less disastrous than preventive war."[92]

Many Israeli political, military, and intelligence experts also oppose a preventive attack on Iran, at least until Israel is left with no other option. The former chief of Mossad, Israel's foreign intelligence agency, Meir Dagan has famously said that attacking Iran's nuclear installations was "the stupidest thing I have ever heard," that an Israeli attack could at most delay the program, and that Israel "would not withstand a regional conflict ignited by such an attack."[93] Dagan subsequently apologized for his harsh language, but reaffirmed that an attack on Iran's nuclear program would be foolish and futile, and should be undertaken only as a "last option."[94] Other Israeli officials believe that a preventive attack may be beyond Israel's capacity to conduct effectively, at least from the air,[95] could require troops on the ground, would solidify popular support for the Islamic regime, and could cause Iran to decide definitively to use the capacities it has achieved to develop nuclear weapons at secret, protected sites with no inspections allowed.[96] Yuval Diskin, former head of Israel's Shin Bet intelligence service, said he had "no faith" in the ability of the current government to handle the Iranian threat, because they make decisions based on "messianic feelings."[97]

Government officials in Israel have criticized these statements, primarily on the ground that they undercut the potential threat of an attack.[98] Vice-Prime Minister Moshe Yaalon has said, for example, that questioning the wisdom of Israel's ability to attack Iran's nuclear program sends Iran the wrong message: "As long as the Iranians are not convinced that there is the political stomach to execute such an attack they will continue with their manipulations. Today the Iranian regime thinks this stomach is not there, whether as a military attack or sanctions."[99] He and others believe that a strike against Iranian nuclear facilities would be difficult but would not set off "widespread acts of terrorism and sky-high oil prices."[100] Israeli officials and supporters have pressed the view that delaying a decision on attacking Iran will soon create what Minister Ehud Barak calls an "immunity stage" in which the option of a preventive attack is precluded by the use of deep bunkers and other adjustments.[101] They have sought from the US what Amos Yadlin has described as "an ironclad American assurance that if Israel refrains from acting in its own window of opportunity—and all other options have failed to halt Tehran's nuclear quest—Washington will act to prevent a nuclear Iran while it is still within its power to do so."[102] In his book *Israeli Statecraft*, Professor Yehezkel Dror states: "Israel certainly wants other countries to prevent Iran from having nuclear weapons, and is surely using the possibility of an Israeli attack on Iran as one of the means to convince them to do so."[103] Iranian officials undoubtedly see the US statements as intended to satisfy Israel's need for reassurance, in order to keep Israel from attacking.

While President Obama has shifted his rhetorical position toward the official Israeli view that Iran must be prevented from obtaining nuclear weapons by force if necessary,[104] it is nonetheless impossible to know with certainty whether the US (or for that matter, Israel) will at any point actually launch preventive attacks on Iran's nuclear program.[105] Doubts regarding the balance of costs and benefits of preventively attacking Iran remain, especially in the US (and Israeli) military,[106] and they result, not from any lack of agreement on the seriousness of the threat posed by Iran's nuclear program, but from the difficulties, potential futility, and adverse consequences of such an attack, and from differences as to whether a nuclear-armed Iran could be deterred from using or threatening the use of nuclear weapons. As in the case of North Korea, the USSR, and China, the disadvantages of a preventive military campaign aimed at keeping Iran denuclearized are real.[107]

An Alternative to Preventive Attack and Containment

This book presents an alternative to the options of preventive attack and containment, one that would reverse the current policy of tolerating IRGC aggression, test whether Iran can in fact be deterred, and set the stage for constructive negotiations based on strength and effective diplomatic practices. Based on current projections in the

Iran Project report, Iran may be able to enrich enough uranium to produce a single nuclear weapon in four months, and to develop a weapon and the means of delivering it in one and two years respectively.[108] The utility of an alternative approach can therefore be determined without losing the option of a preventive attack.

The changes in policy required are straightforward and long overdue. First, the US must broaden its response to Iran—beyond attempting to deal with the exceptionally difficult *prospective* threat posed by its nuclear program to include addressing the relatively manageable *present* threat posed by IRGC surrogate and terrorist attacks. The IRGC has a thirty-year record of aggression against the US, and the latter's failure to defend itself against that aggression has long been a fundamental shortcoming of US national security policy. Allowing IRGC aggression to go unanswered has undermined US credibility and enabled the IRGC and its allies in the Iranian government to pursue their radical objectives at minimal cost and with increased domestic and international stature and influence. Defensive actions against appropriate IRGC targets could not be characterized as "unprovoked." They would be lawful, legitimate, and effective, and would increase the costs to Iran of continuing to support IRGC surrogate and terrorist attacks against US forces, nationals, and interests. Moreover, the pressure generated by this policy would increase the prospect of Iran deciding to negotiate in earnest, in order to stabilize its international relations and ultimately reduce the threat posed by its nuclear program.

As increased US strength in defending against IRGC aggression leads Iran to seek genuine engagement, the US should engage Iran in the same manner the Reagan Administration engaged the Soviet Union. The failure of US efforts to engage Iran successfully over the last thirty years is directly related to its failure to respond firmly to IRGC aggression. Instead of responding firmly, as it did to Soviet interventions and misconduct, the US has refused to negotiate with

Iran, making effective engagement impossible. To bring about the fruitful negotiations needed to curb both the IRGC's aggressive conduct and its nuclear intentions, the US should confront IRGC aggression directly and negotiate with Iran in accordance with practices that have proved effective in dealing with a belligerent, ideologically driven enemy.

CHAPTER 2

Thirty Years of IRGC Aggression

IRGC support for surrogate and terrorist attacks against the US has continued unchecked for over thirty years. Since 1983, IRGC-sponsored operations have caused the deaths of at least 1,000 American soldiers, as well as many members of other armed forces and thousands of non-combatants, including Iraqis, Afghanis, Lebanese, Palestinians, Israelis, Saudis, and Argentineans. Since initiating its Patterns of Global Terrorism Report in 1993, the US State Department has judged Iran—especially its IRGC—to be the world's most dangerous state sponsor of terrorism every year. In 2007, under Executive Order 13382, the State Department designated the IRGC as a proliferator of weapons of mass destruction.[1] Simultaneously, under Executive Order 13224, the Treasury Department named the IRGC-Quds Force as a supporter of terrorism.[2] No other foreign government agency or state has received such a US-government designation.

The authority and roles of the IRGC have increased significantly since its creation. In addition to its activities in protecting the Islamic revolution from foreign influences, the IRGC has some 125,000 members who have taken on major national security, defense, and domestic roles, and it operates and profits from a broad range of business interests. Its military forces are parallel to and by now more important than Iran's regular armed forces; it has its own army, navy, and air force, as well as the Quds Force, whose members are trained to infiltrate and assassinate people in foreign countries.[3] The IRGC controls Iran's ballistic missile programs and, in conjunction with the Grand Ayatollah, the nuclear program as well. Its generals are appointed by the Grand Ayatollah, rather than by the president or speaker of the Majlis (legislature), and former IRGC members hold many key ministerial positions in the government. IRGC components operate on university campuses and other places where they ferret out resistance to the Islamic government; particularly notorious is the Basij Force, whose responsibilities include enforcing Islamic standards of dress and behavior. The IRGC has increased its wealth and commercial power through smuggling and by obtaining government awards of no-bid contracts. It is widely seen as corrupt.[4]

Iran vehemently protests the accusations that it is a state sponsor of terrorism, and routinely blames the US and "the Zionist entity" for spreading lies about its activities. Those denials have been rejected not only by the US but also by most other governments and by courts in several countries that have found IRGC officials and other Iranians guilty of murder and other major crimes. In fact, while Iran denies being involved in "terrorism" against or within other states, it cites a long-discredited definition of "terrorism" that would allow it to use force illegally to advance the "religious and revolutionary values of the Iranian people," including its right to support oppressed people such as the Sadrists, Hezbollah, and Hamas.[5] Its former "moderate" President Mohammed Khatami explained Iran's position as it applies to Israel in terms that terrorist groups and their supporters have traditionally invoked: "Defending the land and expelling occupation is resistance while terrorism is occupation of land and ousting its inhabitants and this is what Israel is doing."[6] The UN has officially rejected any definition of "terrorism" that would allow a state to intervene in armed conflicts, or deliberately or unreasonably to attack, kill, and injure non-combatants.[7] As Dr. Abbas Milani has explained, Iran's claims are similar to the Brezhnev Doctrine's assertion of moral superiority and revolutionary entitlement, and its methods closely resemble those employed by the Soviets in pursuing their goals.[8] The record of IRGC aggression is overwhelming.

Lebanon

The IRGC helped organize Hezbollah in 1982 and has since provided its members with "structure, training, material support, moral guidance, and often operational direction."[9] Hezbollah attacks on Americans began after July 4, 1982, when three Iranian diplomats and a journalist disappeared at a Maronite-controlled crossing in Lebanon. Two weeks later, David Dodge, president of the American University of Beirut, was seized and held, the first of several Americans taken hostage by groups supported by Iran. The IRGC also trained the Hezbollah terrorists who conducted the 1983 attacks on the US Embassy and Marine barracks in Beirut, which resulted in the deaths of 264 Americans.[10] (France lost fifty-eight soldiers in a suicide attack on the same day, and Israel lost sixty people two days later.) IRGC operatives taught the attackers how to carry out suicide bombings and other types of assaults, and supplied them with equipment and explosives. In planning these attacks, the IRGC worked with Imad Mugniyah, a Lebanese Shiite who went on to become a Hezbollah military commander and a major figure in Lebanese and Syrian-based terrorist activities against the US and Israel.

Seizures and murders of Americans in Lebanon continued in 1984. Malcolm Kerr, president of the American University of Beirut, was seized and murdered in 1984.[11] William Buckley, chief of the intelligence section in the US embassy in Beirut, was abducted two months later, tortured repeatedly, and finally killed in June 1985.[12] Meanwhile, in September 1984, Iran teamed with Hezbollah to bomb the US embassy annex in Beirut, killing twenty-four, including two American servicemen.[13] In *Brewer v. Islamic Republic of Iran*, a US district court found that the Islamic Republic of Iran, the Ministry of Information and Security of Iran (MOIS), and the IRGC provided "material support and resources" for the embassy bombing.[14] The court concluded that the perpetrators were the "militant Islamic fundamentalist Shi'ite organization known as Hezbollah, . . . an agency or instrumentality of the Iranian MOIS."[15] These findings were confirmed in a later case, *Welch v. Islamic Republic of Iran*, where satellite reconnaissance photos revealed "an identical, life-size model of the Embassy Annex in the training camps in the Bekaa Valley."[16]

In June 1985, Imad Mugniyah, acting on behalf of Hezbollah, helped plan and implement the hijacking of TWA 847; US Navy diver Robert Stethem was murdered on television, his body dumped from the plane to the tarmac below. During the hijacking, two of Mugniyah's men publicly praised the virtues of the Shiite revolution in Iran.[17] Mugniyah actually boarded Flight 847 at one point in the hostage process and may have been present for the interrogation of American military personnel who were removed from the plane after its arrival in Beirut.[18] There is some debate over which Lebanese terrorist group carried out the hijacking of TWA 847; but Iran's involvement and influence in the affair was confirmed by American intelligence sources, which established that the Iranian government ordered Hezbollah in Beirut to bring the crisis to an end.[19]

International intelligence experts identified Mugniyah as the mastermind behind many major terrorist acts by Hezbollah during the 1980s and 1990s. His connection to Iran remained close. A 2006 report concluded: "Mugniyah appears to operate as a bridge between Iran and Hezbollah, working for both and calibrating their agendas."[20] *New Yorker* foreign affairs reporter Jeffrey Goldberg stated in 2002: "It is believed that Mugniyah takes orders from the office of Iran's supreme leader, Ayatollah Khamenei, but that he reports to a man named Gassim Soleimani, the chief of a branch of the Iranian Revolutionary Guard Corps called Al Quds or the Jerusalem Force."[21] Mugniyah's connection to Hezbollah dates back to the early 1980s, when he worked as a bodyguard for Sayyid Muhammad Fadlallah,

Hezbollah's spiritual leader. A 1996 classified assessment paper compiled by Israeli Military Intelligence concluded that Iran had chosen to take an indirect course in attacking Israel and that this course went through Mugniyah.[22] British intelligence sources also maintained that Mugniyah supplied funds from Iran to the Palestinian Islamic Jihad.[23] He is believed to have sought refuge in Iran on multiple occasions and to have applied for Iranian citizenship in 1985.[24] In one analyst's view: "One must regard Mugniyah as someone who is on the margins. In other words he believes in Hezbollah's ideology and Iranian-styled goals, but he is not their agent. In fact, Mugniyah does not report to Hezbollah, but to the Iranians."[25]

Iraq

IRGC-supported attacks on US troops in Iraq began soon after the US overthrew Saddam Hussein in 2002 and continued after they left at the end of 2011. A 2006 Congressional Research Service report concluded that Iran supplied C-4 explosives found on Shiite militiamen.[26] A 2009 CRS report found: "On February 11, 2007, U.S. military briefers in Baghdad provided what they said was specific evidence that Iran had supplied armor-piercing 'explosively formed projectiles' (EFPs) to Shiite (Sadrist) militiamen . . . responsible for over 200 U.S. combat deaths since 2003."[27] Brigadier General Kevin Begner reported that Lebanese Hezbollah members were assisting the IRGC's Quds Force in aiding Iraqi Shiite militias and that, based on the testimony of then-Sadr aide Qais al-Khazali and Hezbollah operative Ali Musa Daqduq, "Iran gives about $3 million per month to these Iraqi militias."[28] According to a 2010 CRS report, twenty Quds Force officers were arrested in Iraq between December 2006 and October 2007.[29] In July 2011, *The Washington Post* reported that, two years earlier, US troops had discovered a cache of weapons whose contents included "150 copper plates that had been professionally milled for use in a particularly deadly type of device known as 'explosively formed projectile' bombs" as well as "sophisticated launching rails for rockets that are designed to increase range and accuracy." This cache was "linked to an Iraqi militia that U.S. officials say is trained and equipped by Iran."[30]

In July 2011, Chairman of the Joint Chiefs of Staff Admiral Michael Mullen confirmed that Iranian high-tech weapons, "which are killing our troops,"[31] were "very directly" being provided by Iran to Shiite extremists in Iraq. Secretary of Defense Leon Panetta said four days later that "We are very concerned about Iran and the weapons they are providing to extremists here in Iraq. . . . In June we lost a hell of a lot of Americans as a result of those attacks."[32] US forensic teams "traced the origins of an improvised rocket-assisted mortar (IRAM) used by an Iraqi extremist to the Quds Force, part of the Iranian Revolutionary Guard."[33] The US ambassador to Iraq, James F. Jeffrey, said, also in July 2011: "There is no doubt this is Iranian. We're seeing more lethal weapons, more accurate weapons, more longer-range weapons. And we're seeing more sophisticated mobile and other deployment options, and we're seeing better-trained people." General Lloyd Austin, Commander of US forces in Iraq, said on the same day that advanced weapons "are coming in from Iran, we're certain of that."[34] The US has compiled substantial evidence that many Iraqis were taken to Iran for training by cadres of the IRGC and Hezbollah in techniques for attacking US forces.[35]

The weakness with which US officials reacted to IRGC supported attacks on the US in Iraq is detailed in the recent book, *The Endgame*, written by Michael R. Gordon and Lieutenant General (ret.) Bernard Trainor. The book sets out the abundant evidence of Iranian supply to forces bent on disrupting US objectives and killing three Shiite enemies: US troops, British troops, and Sunni combatants. It makes clear how well aware the US commanders and diplomats were of IRGC involvement, led by Quds Force Commander, Qasem Suleimani.[36] After US forces managed to seize some IRGC personnel, including the Lebanese IRGC-backed militants Qais al-Khazali and

Ali Musa Daqduq, Suleimani sent a message through an Iraqi intelligence official that attacks on Americans would be reduced "dramatically" if al-Khazali were re-leased. General David Petraeus reportedly told Secretary of Defense Gates that he "was considering telling the president that I believe Iran is, in fact, waging war on the United States in Iraq"; Petraeus also sent a message to the Quds Force that the US would "drastically escalate their raids against the Quds Force's suspected proxies and agents in Iraq—raids that would involve Task Force 17, a secret commando unit dedicated to countering Iranian influence."

Michael Gordon apparently accepts that this threat led the Quds Force to stop attacks on Americans for "more than a year," but even if this unsubstantiated statement is correct, he acknowledges that the attacks resumed and continued until the US withdrew from Iraq in 2011.[37] The fact is that, while Petraeus and the Bush Administration refused to talk to Suleimani, they ended up doing what he wanted by releasing al-Khazali (in exchange for the release of a British computer consultant)[38] and turning Daqduq over to the Iraqi government—despite the clear risk that Iraq would release him on the basis that he had violated no Iraqi law by helping to kill American soldiers.[39] Upon his release, al-Khazali resumed his leadership of the militia Asaib al-Haq, and he recently issued a threat to attack US interests in Iraq because of a cartoon film that insulted the Prophet Muhammad.[40]

Afghanistan

Iran had an adversarial relationship with the Taliban, and after 2002 took steps to improve relations with Persian-speaking members of the Northern Alliance. It cooperated with the US in helping to establish the current Afghan government.

After unsuccessfully seeking to engage the US more broadly, however, Iran helped to reestablish Gulbuddin Hekmatyar as a Taliban warlord in western Afghanistan. Hekmatyar is committed to under-mining the Kabul government and killing NATO soldiers.[41] The IRGC has provided members of the Taliban with improvised explosive devices (IEDs)[42] and powerful rockets that have increased the number of NATO casualties.[43] Pentagon officials, who describe the rockets as roughly doubling the range at which the Taliban can attack NATO forces, have concluded that their markings and location provide a "high degree" of confidence that they came from the Quds Force.[44] A recent State Department report on Iranian support for international terrorism states: "Iran's Quds Force provided training to the Taliban in Afghanistan on small unit tactics, small arms, explosives, and indirect fire weapons. Since at least 2006, Iran has arranged arms shipments to select Taliban members, including small arms and associated ammunition, rocket-propelled grenades, mortar rounds, 107 mm rockets, and plastic explosives."[45]

In May 2010, General Stanley A. McChrystal, then commander of US and NATO forces in Afghanistan, told reporters that Iran was providing material help to the Taliban. In response to Iran's direct involvement, McChrystal commented: "The training that we have seen occurs inside Iran with fighters moving inside Iran. . . . The weapons that we have received come from Iran into Afghanistan."[46] In August 2010, the Treasury Department specifically described Iran's IRGC-Quds Force as "the Government of Iran's support for terrorism and terrorist organizations, including . . . the Taliban" and named senior members of the IRGC as providing "financial and material support to the Taliban."[47] Additionally, the department concluded, the Quds Force "provides select members of the Taliban with weapons, funding, logistics, and training" in Afghanistan, indicating that their involvement goes beyond simply supplying weapons. More recently, the Treasury Department imposed sanctions on the IRGC for allowing drug trafficking through Iran from Afghan sources.[48] Under Secretary for Terrorism and Financial Intelligence David S. Cohen stated, "Today's action exposes IRGC-QF involvement in trafficking narcotics, made doubly reprehensible here because it is done as part of a broader scheme to support terrorism."[49]

As the US prepares to withdraw from Afghanistan, Iran is increasing its efforts to influence, if not overthrow, the national government in Kabul. General H.R. McMaster, who played key roles in the wars in both Iraq and Afghanistan, believes that Iran "is pressuring Kabul to reject the Strategic Partnership Agreement" between Afghanistan and the US, and using its ownership or control over many media outlets, as well as its funding of schools, to influence policy.[50] Although these are lawful activities, they reflect the purpose behind Iran's illegal supply of arms and training: to side with the Taliban in undermining US efforts to support the Kabul government.

Saudi Arabia

The IRGC has been responsible for many attacks against the Saudi government. Its most significant action aimed at Americans in Saudi Arabia was its support for the bombing of the Khobar Towers barracks, in which nineteen US Air Force personnel were killed and 372 wounded.[51] An indictment of those responsible for the bombing, filed in the US in June 2001, named thirteen Saudis and one Lebanese as defendants; but it also explicitly alleged that Saudi Hezbollah, the organization that conducted the bombing, was "inspired, supported, and directed by various elements of the government of Iran."[52] Federal Bureau of Investigation (FBI) Director Louis Freeh summed up the evidence developed as to Iran's role in a *Wall Street Journal* op-ed in June 2006:

> [T]he bombers admitted they had been trained by the Iranian external security service (IRGC) in the Bekaa Valley, and received their passports at the Iranian Embassy in Damascus, along with $250,000 cash for the operation from IRGC Gen. Ahmad Sharifi. We later

learned that senior members of the Iranian government, including Ministry of Defense, Ministry of Intelligence and Security (MOIS), and the Spiritual Leader's office had selected Khobar as their target and commissioned the Saudi Hezbollah to carry out the operation.

Iranian involvement in the attack has been questioned.[53] The evidence of IRGC involvement, however, is strong, and at least one US federal court has specifically held the IRGC responsible.[54]

United States

Iranian support for attacks aimed at the US began with the seizure of the US embassy and its diplomatic staff in Tehran in November 1979. The Ayatollah Khomeini supported this seizure by religious students and held the diplomats hostage for 444 days, despite orders for their release by the UNSC and the International Court of Justice (ICJ) (both in December 1979). The US hostages were harassed, beaten, and mistreated in many ways.[55]

Iran's cooperation with al-Qaeda is an important aspect of its support for attacks on the US. In its 1998 indictment of Osama bin Laden, the US noted that he had called for al-Qaeda to "put aside its differences with Shi'ite Muslim terrorist organizations, including the government of Iran and its affiliated terror group Hezbollah, to cooperate against the perceived common enemy, the United States and its allies."[56] According to the 9/11 Commission, eight of the ten hijackers responsible for the 9/11 attacks passed through Iran between October 2000 and February 2001. The commission's final report found that in the early 1990s "senior al-Qaeda operatives and trainers traveled to Iran to receive training in explosives" and that "in the fall of 1993, another such delegation went to the Bekaa Valley in Lebanon for further training in explosives as well as intelligence and security."[57]

Among those receiving Hezbollah training was an Egyptian, Saif al-Adel, chief of al-Qaeda's military operations. Al-Adel was a leading figure in the attacks on US embassies in Africa, after which he reportedly sought refuge in Iran. In 2002, in what some believe to be a response to President Bush's "Axis of Evil" speech, Iran transferred sixteen suspected al-Qaeda officials to Saudi Arabia.[58] These individuals told Saudi interrogators that Iran had asked them to leave, while allowing other, more important al-Qaeda leaders to stay.[59] Early in 2003, Iran admitted having some al-Qaeda leaders in custody, but would not identify them.[60] According to US and Saudi intelligence officials, al-Adel was among those detained in Iran, under house arrest in the custody of the IRGC.[61] From his sanctuary in Iran, al-Adel continued communicating with the al-Qaeda cell in Saudi Arabia and advised al-Qaeda operatives who conducted a 2003 truck-bomb attack at housing complexes for Western nationals in Riyadh; thirty-six people were killed, including nine Americans.[62]

Intelligence experts believe that, in addition to Saif al-Adel, Iran gave refuge to some 200 al-Qaeda members. When the US demanded that Iran extradite those responsible for the Riyadh bombings, Iran sarcastically countered by offering to give up al-Qaeda people in exchange for members of the Mujehidin e-Khalk (MEK), an anti-Iranian group that the Clinton Administration put on the State Department list of terrorist organizations in an effort to establish better relations with Iran. MEK members were subsequently given refuge in Iraq after they gave up terrorist methods; they later supplied the US with information that revealed important Iranian nuclear program activities.[63] On September 28, 2012, the State Department announced it had removed the MEK from its list of states that support terrorism after a litigation in which the MEK established that it had renounced terrorism, had not engaged in such acts for over a decade, and was cooperating with the United States.[64]

A letter intercepted in 2008 revealed that al-Qaeda's current chief, Ayman al-Zawahiri, "thanked the leadership of Iran's Revolutionary

Guards for providing assistance to al-Qaeda to set up its terrorist network in Yemen." Al-Qaeda in Yemen conducted ten attacks during 2011, including two bombings at the American Embassy.[65] Zawahiri noted that, without Iran's "monetary and infrastructure assistance," it would not have been possible for al-Qaeda to establish new bases in Yemen after it had been forced to abandon much of its infrastructure in Iraq and Saudi Arabia.

According to US officials, Iran is currently "allowing the country to be used as a transit point for funneling money and people from the Persian Gulf to Pakistan and Afghanistan."[66] Under Secretary of the Treasury Cohen said in July 2011: "By exposing Iran's secret deal with al-Qaeda allowing it to funnel funds and operatives through its territory, we are illuminating yet another aspect of Iran's unmatched support for terrorism."[67] Among the six people upon whom the US Treasury imposed sanctions on account of this activity is Atiyah Abd al-Rahman, believed to be the second in command of al-Qaeda and based in Pakistan.[68] Iran's support is helping al-Qaeda recover from US operations that killed its leader Osama bin Laden and others.

On October 11, 2011, the US filed a criminal complaint charging Manssor Arbabsiar, an Iranian American, and Gholam Shakuri, an Iranian member of the Quds Force of the IRGC, with conspiring to kill Adel al-Jubeir, the Saudi ambassador to the US, in a bombing planned to take place in downtown Washington, DC. In a classified cable released by WikiLeaks in April 2008, Ambassador al-Jubeir was quoted as reminding US officials of King Abdullah's "frequent exhortations to the U.S. to attack Iran and so put an end to its nuclear weapons program. . . . ' He told you to cut off the head of the snake,' Jubeir was reported to have said."[69] Iranian Foreign Minister Ali-Akbar Salehi dismissed the US charges as "so funny that is not justifiable even to a child," accusing the US government of concocting the scheme "to divert public opinion from problems that the US, international Zionism, and the West are facing" as a result of the costs of the wars in Iraq and Afghanistan and demonstrations due to "widening of poverty."[70] But the complaint contains significant details that have not been rebutted, the action alleged is similar to other IRGC assassinations of enemies in foreign countries, and additional evidence appears to leave open only the question whether this IRGC operation was approved at the highest level of the Iranian government.

Arbabsiar allegedly arranged with an FBI confidential source to hire a drug cartel in Mexico to conduct the bombing as the first of several assignments in exchange for $1.5 million, which he told the informant "was in Iran." Arbabsiar said he had been asked to recruit someone to conduct the bombing by his cousin, a "big general" in the IRGC who had worked in "other countries" for the Iranian government. A down payment of $100,000 was sent from a foreign entity by wire through a bank in New York to a "UC Bank" account specified by the confidential informant. Arbabsiar described his co-defendant, Shakuri, as a colonel in the Quds Force. He recorded several conversations with Shakuri after he was arrested and agreed to cooperate. In them, Shakuri indicated that others involved in the plot wanted the bombing to take place promptly. He promised to pay the full agreed-on amount after the bombing had taken place, and told Arbabsiar to allow his own person to be used as the guaranty for payment. On October 17, 2012, Arbabsiar pleaded guilty to conspiring with senior members of the Quds Force to murder Ambassador al-Jubeir in a Washington, DC, restaurant.[71]

The IRGC assassination scheme is consistent with the murders of "enemies" of Iran arranged by the IRGC in Paris and Berlin, described below, and would not have been the first such IRGC act in the US. According to the Iran Human Rights Documentation Center, 162 political assassinations were sponsored or carried out by the Islamic Republic of Iran from 1979 to 1999. Two of them took place in the US, involving Ali Akbar Tabatabai in 1980 and Nareh Rafi'zadeh in 1992. Tabatabai served as a diplomat under the Shah, and Rafi'zadeh was the wife and sister-in-law of former intelligence agents.[72] Some individuals have expressed skepticism that Iran would approve what they regard as an amateurish scheme. But the scheme's seeming recklessness may reflect the risks the IRGC is prepared to take in light of continuing US inaction in the face of its attacks on US soldiers and interests.

Additional evidence has established, moreover, that Arbabsiar does in fact have a cousin who is a general in the IRGC, named Abdul Reza Shahlai. He is Shakuri's boss, and he is believed to have coordinated the plot and approved the payments made. The US Treasury Department has named Shahlai, along with four others (including the Quds Force commander Suleimani, who is responsible for the deaths of many American soldiers in Iraq), as conspirators in the bombing attempt, and has imposed sanctions prohibiting any dealings with them by Americans.[73] Shahlai is known to have planned a January 2007 attack by Sadrist forces on US soldiers at Karbala, Iraq, in which five US servicemen were killed.[74] He approached Arbabsiar while the latter was visiting Iran and approved the use of a Mexican drug cartel to do the killing—a suggestion made by Arbabsiar based on his extensive business dealings in Mexico.

The US was lucky that Arbabsiar proposed the IRGC plan to a member of a drug cartel who had agreed to cooperate with the FBI and who recorded their dealings under FBI supervision. FBI Director Robert S. Mueller, III said of the plan: "Though it reads like the pages of a Hollywood movie script, the impact would have been very real, and many lives would have been lost."[75] James Clapper, director of National Intelligence, testified before the Senate Intelligence Committee on January 30, 2012 that the plot to assassinate the Saudi ambassador indicates that some Iranian officials—"probably including Supreme Leader Ali Khamenei—have changed their calculus and are now more willing to conduct an attack in the United States in response to real or perceived actions that threaten the regime."[76]

Attacks on Other States

As reflected in US State Department reports, the IRGC has directly engaged in or supported a variety of terrorist actions against (and sometimes within) other foreign states. Iran has encouraged and supported Shia groups in Bahrain, Iraq, Lebanon, and Saudi Arabia in a manner analogous to the Soviet Union's efforts to spread communist ideology. It assisted the ad-Dawa group's 1983 attack on the American embassy and other targets in Kuwait, killing relatively few people only because the explosives used were not properly rigged; Imad Mugniyah's brother-in-law was among the 17 terrorists arrested.[77]

Iran has also assassinated many former Iranian officials or dissidents living or traveling in other countries. These actions have apparently been based on a policy established by the Ayatollah Khomeini who at his death is said to have left a list of some five hundred Iranians to be killed as enemies of Islam.[78] In 1991, for example, Iranian agents assassinated former Prime Minister Shapour Bakhtiar in Paris; two of the three men charged, both associated with the IRGC, were convicted. In September 1992, in an action arranged by the Iranian Minister of Intelligence, Ali Fallahian, four Iranian Kurdish opponents of Iran's Islamic regime were killed in the Mykonos restaurant in Berlin. The German courts convicted four of the five defendants charged, including Fallahian, and found that the assassinations had been ordered by the "Committee for Special Operations" consisting of the Grand Ayatollah Khamenei, President Rafsanjani, and other officials.[79] In 1995, Iran aided an unsuccessful effort to assassinate President Hosni Mubarak of Egypt while he was on a trip to Ethiopia.[80]

Not surprisingly, the IRGC and its Quds Force have participated actively in attacks on Israel. The organizations support several terrorist groups in Gaza and the West Bank, including the Palestine Liberation Organization, Hamas, Islamic Jihad, and the Popular Front for the Liberation of Palestine,[81] providing weapons that have fueled the Palestinian/Israel conflict and its attendant terrorist attacks. Israel captured a ship, the *Karine A*, in January 2002, in the midst of the second *intifada*, loaded in Iran with 50 tons of weapons for the Palestinian Authority, then under Yasser Arafat.[82] In March 2011, the Israeli navy intercepted the cargo ship *Victoria* carrying 50 tons of weapons from Iran for Hamas in Gaza.[83] In addition to conventional light arms, the cargo included six C-704 anti-ship missiles that would have enabled Hamas to target Israeli shipping and recently established offshore gas platforms, posing a serious threat to Israel's security and economy.

The IRGC has also given extensive assistance to Lebanese terrorists in their attacks on Israel. It supplied thousands of rockets that Hezbollah fired into Israel during the 2006 war.[84] In November 2006, Israel intercepted a shipment of arms from Iran to Hezbollah in Lebanon, aboard the MV *Francop*, a cargo ship flying the Antiguan flag. The ship had three dozen containers filled with arms, including 2,800 rockets, all in polyethylene sacks with English and Farsi markings, establishing that the sacks were made by Iran's Petrochemical Co.[85] Turkey has intercepted at least two shipments of arms believed to be from Iran and intended for delivery to Syria for Hezbollah in Lebanon.[86] In January 2009, Cypriot authorities captured a Cypriot ship that contained anti-tank weapons, artillery, and rocket-manufacturing equipment believed to be bound for Hezbollah in Lebanon.[87] Israel claims that during its 2006 conflict in Lebanon, Iranian commandos assisting Hezbollah launched an anti-ship missile from Lebanon that struck an Israeli naval vessel, killing four sailors.[88]

Since 2006, Iran has armed Hezbollah even more heavily, in violation of UN Security Council Resolution 1701. Iran has provided Hezbollah with over 50,000 rockets, including some that can reach the northern suburbs of Tel Aviv. Iran appears to treat Lebanon as its first line of defense against Israel; the IRGC air force commander, General Amir Ali Hagizadeh, expressed pride in Iran's ability to deploy enough missiles to enable Hezbollah to increase the number and range fired at Israel even as the 2006 war progressed.[89]

Iranian diplomats, as well as other high-ranking officials in the IRGC, assisted Hezbollah in the Buenos Aires bombings of the Israeli Embassy and Jewish Community Center, incidents discussed in greater detail below.[90] In December 2011, US District Judge John D. Bates ruled that, although the bombings of the US embassies in Kenya and Tanzania were conducted by al-Qaeda, they could not have been accomplished without the "direct assistance" of Iran, which "aided, abetted and conspired with Hezbollah, Osama Bin Laden, and al-Qaeda."[91] The IRGC is also suspected of training and possibly supporting al-Qaeda attackers who bombed two synagogues in Istanbul in November 2003.[92]

Interference with Navigational Rights

Iran has deliberately interfered with navigational rights in the Persian Gulf. During its war with Iraq, Iran threatened and attacked Kuwaiti and other vessels, and mined the Gulf. The US responded to these actions in 1988 by sinking several Iranian navy vessels and IRGC speedboats, and destroying oil platforms being used as part of Iran's mining operations, as described below.

Iran has continued periodically to challenge US public and other foreign vessels in the Gulf, sometimes forcing US commanders to change course to avoid encounters. US commanders have complained about deliberate IRGC interference with navigational freedom in the area but have not been permitted to respond in a manner calculated to deter it.[93] Admiral James A. Lyons (Ret.), former commander of the US Pacific Fleet, has recounted that while he was commander of US naval forces in the Gulf, IRGC-controlled ships simulated close attacks on US Navy vessels. He believes that tolerating such IRGC interference is "conditioning our naval forces to allow Iranian naval craft and ships to get dangerously close, which is a clear formula for disaster." Lyons called for the navy's rules of engagement to be changed in order to prevent a "close-in attack."[94]

On January 3, 2012, as US Navy vessels departed the Gulf during Iranian naval exercises, Iran's chief of staff declared that the US should keep its vessels out of the area, threatening to close the Straits of Hormuz to all oil tankers if an embargo on Iranian oil were imposed.[95] The US rejected that threat and sent warships back into the Gulf. Secretary of Defense Panetta announced, in an interview on January 8, 2012, that the US would not tolerate Iranian interference with the passage of international commerce through the Gulf.[96] Iran has thus far made no effort to exclude US naval vessels. IRGC naval forces, however, are more reckless and unprofessional than the regular Iranian navy, and the US may again be challenged by IRGC speedboats or threatened by the missiles it controls.

On November 1, 2012, fighter planes "under the command of the Iranian Revolutionary Guard Corps, whose activities are routinely more aggressive than those of the conventional Iranian Air Force," fired at an unarmed US surveillance drone the US claims was flying in international airspace. While this situation is not strictly analogous to IRGC interference with US vessels in the Gulf, the attack represents an escalation in IRGC confrontation. The US reportedly sent a strong protest concerning this attack to Iran through the Swiss government, noting that it would not halt such surveillance activities. But the US government took no other action.[97]

CHAPTER 3

Thirty Years of US Weakness

I f strength and effective diplomacy go hand-in-hand in dealing with an enemy, as Secretary Shultz has observed, the US failure to defend itself against thirty years of IRGC aggression may well explain why the US has been unable to engage the Islamic Republic effectively.

The classic, modern American example of strength and effective diplomacy was the strategy initiated by President Harry Truman as part of the Cold War and carried forward with substantial bi-partisan consistency. As nuclear powers capable of mutual assured destruction, both states were limited in the measures they could adopt in order to prevent misunderstandings or uncertainties. Beyond these restraints, however, most US presidents energetically countered Soviet efforts to influence and intimidate other states.

President Reagan and his UN ambassador, Jeanne Kirkpatrick, responded to the Brezhnev Doctrine (holding that the Soviet Union was entitled to spread "socialism" by assisting in the overthrow of non-socialist governments) with the Reagan Doctrine (holding that the US had the right to attempt to prevent Soviet-inspired and -supported revolutions).[1] Reagan's Administration implemented the Reagan Doctrine in several places, including Granada, Nicaragua, El Salvador, Honduras, Afghanistan, and Angola.[2] In each, the

Administration either used force or supported locals in using it to prevent the overthrow of regimes by groups seeking to impose Soviet-aligned governments. In Afghanistan, US assistance enabled Mujahedeen fighters to attack Soviet forces seeking to keep their puppet ruler in power, resulting in the deaths and injuries of many Soviet soldiers, and ultimately forcing the Soviet Union to withdraw. The US strengthened its armed forces, deployed intermediate-range missiles in Europe in response to their deployment by the Soviets, and began to pursue ballistic missile defense, an effort the Soviets could not afford to match. The US also used "soft power"—through Voice of America broadcasts, exchange programs, and other overt and non-violent covert activities—to influence the Soviet public in favor of US positions in the superpower competition then underway.

These policies helped to deter Soviet aggression and convinced the Soviet government to negotiate solutions to conflicts. They also gave the Reagan Administration the credibility necessary to enable Secretary of State Shultz to gain congressional support for negotiating with a state that regularly acted reprehensibly. Without this credibility, diplomatic engagement with the Soviets would have been seen as evidence of weakness. Strength was therefore the indispensable foundation, not only for deterring the Soviets but also for enabling the US to conduct effective diplomacy.

In contrast to the relatively consistent Cold War policy for dealing with the Soviet Union, the US has followed entirely different and inconsistent policies in dealing with the Islamic Republic of Iran. Since the Carter Administration, the US has responded to Iranian aggression with ineffective sanctions and empty warnings and condemnations. The US has employed military action to defend itself against IRGC aggression only once in 30 years—in the Persian Gulf in 1987 and 1988, after attacks on US-flagged vessels and the mining of Gulf waters. No US president has responded to IRGC aggression with actions calculated to convey a clear message to Iran that the US is determined to stop that organization's support for surrogate and terrorist attacks on the US and its interests.

President Jimmy Carter

President Carter's policies toward Iran included at least two actions that had positive consequences. First, as advised by White House Counsel Lloyd Cutler, the president acted timely and effectively in freezing Iranian assets (some $10 billion) in the US. This measure ultimately enabled the Administration, through negotiations in a variety of channels, to secure release of the US hostages in Tehran. In addition, the president maintained the US commitment to free access and use of the Persian Gulf by issuing, in January 1980, what became known as the Carter Doctrine. It made clear that free access was an "essential interest" of the US and that Iranian interference would be countered militarily if necessary.[3]

In other respects, however, the president's statements and actions in dealing with Iran conveyed weakness. His initial reaction to the seizure of the American embassy in Tehran, along with sixty-six diplomats and staff, seemed intended above all to make clear that his administration wanted to avoid resorting to force. He said that he reserved the right to use force to free the hostages but stressed his reluctance to do so: "I'm determined to do the best I can through diplomatic means and through peaceful means to ensure the safety of our hostages and their release. Other actions which I might decide to take would come in the future, after those peaceful means have been exhausted."[4] His administration obtained rulings from the UNSC and the ICJ ordering Iran to release the US hostages; the rulings were ignored.

The president also appealed, directly but fruitlessly, to the Ayatollah Khomeini. He wrote to Khomeini that he was sending two "distinguished Americans," Ramsay Clark (known by then as a radical critic of American foreign policy) and William G. Miller (an Intelligence Committee staff member), to meet with the ayatollah. The envoys' task: to discuss "the situation in Iran and the full range of issues" between the two countries and to seek the immediate release of all Americans "detained" in Tehran for "compelling humanitarian reasons based firmly in international law."[5] Khomeini refused even to meet Clark. Carter also sent his brother, Billy, the owner of a gas station in Plains, Georgia, to Libya to use contacts he had with Muammar Gadhafi to seek help in convincing Iran to free the hostages.

When, after many months of frustrating delay, President Carter did decide to use force, the plan he approved was extremely difficult to implement and failed due to bad weather, accidents, and a lack of adequate preparation and redundancy.[6] Kenneth M. Pollack concluded in his study of modern Iran: "It seems fairly certain that this impression of weakness [conveyed by Carter] contributed to Iran's decision to challenge the United States in Lebanon in the 1980s and early 1990s. . . ." Pollack also relates how in 1979, when Saudi Arabia sought US support under threat from the Iranian revolution, Carter sent a squadron of F-15s but insisted they be unarmed. All that did, Pollack believes, "was convince the Saudis that Washington could not be counted on."[7] This weakness was also apparent in Carter's dealings with the Soviet Union; he declared, for example, that he was "shocked" by its invasion of Afghanistan, despite having received clear warnings of Soviet plans in advance from his ambassador to Russia, Malcolm Toon.[8]

President Ronald Reagan

President Reagan confronted Soviet aggression and promised to combat terrorism without compromise. But he failed to counter IRGC support for surrogate attacks and terrorism with the same determination.

The first major test of the Administration's strength in dealing with IRGC surrogate attacks came with Hezbollah's April 1983 bombing of the US Embassy in Beirut, which killed sixty-three people, including seventeen Americans. The IRGC had trained the attackers and supplied the explosives and equipment used, having by then established, in Eastern Lebanon, bases from which to support Hezbollah's activities. The US took no action in reprisal. Six months later, a suicide-truck bomber crashed into a building being used by US Marines sent to Lebanon to maintain security, killing 241. The IRGC also trained, equipped, and supported the terrorists who carried out this attack. Minutes later, a suicide bombing killed fifty-eight French soldiers in Beirut, and not long afterward another suicide attack killed sixty—including twenty-nine soldiers—at Israel's military headquarters in Tyre.

After the Marine barracks bombing, President Reagan authorized an attack on IRGC bases in Lebanon's Bekaa Valley. The French, convinced of IRGC responsibility for the Beirut attack, sent planes to bomb one of the two IRGC bases President Reagan had authorized as targets. Secretary of Defense Caspar Weinberger managed to derail President Reagan's order, however, arguing that the US did not have clear evidence of IRGC culpability.[9]

Secretary Shultz believed that "it would be devastating" for the US "to cut and run" from Lebanon because of these attacks: "American power must have more to it than a massive deterrent against the Soviets or a relatively simple exercise like Granada."[10] He described the situation in Lebanon as "a low grade war with Iranian and Syrian terrorists," and advocated an antiterrorist force to replace the Marines with expanded rules of engagement and a greater use of naval and air power to assist the Lebanese armed forces. President Reagan approved this plan, but once again Secretary Weinberger intervened and prevailed upon the president to abandon it.[11]

What followed was later described by Shultz as a "virtual stampede" to get out of Lebanon, "far different from my earlier redeployment plan. . . . Our troops left in a rush amid ridicule from the

French and utter disappointment and despair from the Lebanese. . . . I knew then that our staying power under pressure would come into question time and again" due to our "precipitous departure."[12]

The Administration imposed sanctions on Iran and sold arms to Iraq during its war with Iran. But these forms of pressure (along with some covert actions that were undertaken) failed to alter Iran's behavior. Seven US nationals were seized in Lebanon and held hostage for several years by groups associated with Iran. Some Americans, including CIA agent William Buckley, were tortured and killed. Other Hezbollah attacks went unanswered: the April 1984 bombing of a restaurant outside the US Air Force base in Torrejon, Spain (killing eighteen US servicemen); a truck bombing at a temporary annex of the US embassy in Beirut (killing twenty-four); and the murder of two employees of the US Agency for International Development during the hijacking of Kuwait Airways Flight 221 in Tehran (although Iranian forces ultimately stormed the plane, Iran released the hijackers).[13]

My first significant work as legal adviser to the State Department came only days after being sworn in, when, in June 1985, Hezbollah terrorists hijacked TWA 847. Secretary Shultz challenged the heads of all bureaus in the department to come up with options to deal with the crisis. The passengers were being held on the plane, so little could be done without putting their lives in jeopardy. My office nonetheless put together a number of options involving the use of force, creating a flood of protests from other bureaus. At the same time, I supported the terrorists' demand for the release of Lebanese prisoners being held in Israeli prisons in contravention of the Sixth Geneva Convention, the only demand that had merit. The US had repeatedly called on Israel prior to the hijacking to release those prisoners. Department officials were reluctant even to repeat this US position after the hijackers had advanced it as a demand. Israel offered, however, to release the prisoners if the US thought that would help resolve the situation; the White House accepted the offer and passed the information on to Syria. The release of both the prisoners and the hostages followed, but only after Iranian leaders went to Syria and urged them to end the crisis. Once again, no action was taken against Hezbollah or the IRGC for this crime.

The president's frustration over his inability to free the US hostages in Lebanon led ultimately to his Administration's most flagrant instance of weakness in dealing with Iran. In the Iran/Contra affair, the president approved a secret effort for the US to sell Iran weapons in exchange for promises to release the US hostages. High-level American officials flew secretly to Tehran with a cake and a Bible to show the common "roots" of the two cultures in an appeal for a new, mutually beneficial relationship.[14] Three hostages were released after transfers of certain weapons, but three new ones were subsequently seized.[15] When a Lebanese radio station revealed the initiative, those in the Iranian government who had indicated support backed away, forcing an end to the effort. The affair greatly damaged US credibility and put Ali Akbar Rafsanjani, then speaker of the Majlis, on the defensive, since he was considered a principal supporter of the secret negotiation. Rafsanjani's reaction was to heap abuse on the US, calling President Reagan "a doddering old man" with "one foot in the grave" who led a nation "of paper tigers that lacked respect for their elders."[16]

While some Reagan officials were pursuing the release of the US hostages through the sale of arms to Iran, I was leading negotiations for the US in the Iran/US Tribunal in The Hague. I established a working relationship with my counterpart, Gudarz Eftekhar-Jahromi, a member of the Council of Guardians and legal adviser to Speaker Rafsanjani. We were making progress in settling some of the thousands of claims pending before the tribunal. Among these were claims for the release of weapons Iran had paid for but which the US had not delivered at the time of the Islamic revolution. It is amusing in retrospect to recall how Dr. Eftekhar kept pressing me as to why the US would not send Iran weapons it had purchased. He was aware, though I was not, that the US was at that time selling weapons to Iran, and could not understand why we were simultaneously refusing to allow Iran to have weapons for which it had already paid.

Rafsanjani, who had previously called on the US to return Iran's "frozen assets," declared after the secret Iran arms-sales initiative unraveled that the US had no need to engage in hidden dealings with Iran to get its help in securing release of the hostages in Lebanon. All the US had to do was return Iran's assets, and Iran would be happy to assist in getting the US hostages released. He thereafter made this point explicitly and repeatedly, drawing a clear connection between the negotiations in The Hague and Iranian assistance in resolving the hostage problem. For example, the daily report of the Foreign Broadcast Information Service on November 5, 1986, reported Rafsanjani saying that despite Iran's refusal to receive then-former NSC Adviser Robert McFarlane, "if the United States wants Iran to intercede on its behalf in Lebanon 'we have left the door open,' though he stressed that Iranian action on the hostages is conditional on the United States [and France] proving . . . that they are not engaging in 'treason' against Iran and that they are not holding Iranian assets. In return, Iran would ask its Lebanese friends to release the hostages."[17] The *Tehran Times* reported on November 29: "Mr. Rafsanjani made it quite clear that there is no need for direct talks as far as the U.S. is concerned. 'If you deliver our frozen assets which are being held illegally, you can assuredly anticipate our assistance and cooperation with regard to this Lebanon hostage issue.'"[18] He specifically noted on February 27, 1987 that the US was refusing to deliver weapons Iran had paid for and was nonetheless charging Iran for storing the weapons, or selling the weapons to others to make sure Iran did not receive them.[19]

President Rafsanjani's position was reported in the *Washington Post* on April 21, 1987, after he held a news conference in which he complained that the US had overcharged for weapons in the Iran/ Contra Affair and had allowed Israel to become involved even though the US "knows we hate Israel." He "reiterated that his government is still willing to use its influence with radical groups in Lebanon to free western hostages if the United States drops its 'hostile attitude' toward Iran and releases the frozen funds."[20] This Iranian position led some officials in the Administration to resist reaching settlements in The Hague, for fear of appearing to be paying for the release of hostages. But we were able to keep negotiating effectively, and made more progress than had been made in prior years.

President Reagan recovered from the damage inflicted by Iran/Contra through successes in US/Soviet negotiations, and other achievements, including the effective use of force against IRGC aggression in the Gulf during 1987 and 1988. On July 22, 1987, the US-flagged Kuwaiti tanker *Bridgeton* struck a mine laid by the IRGC in its effort to disrupt Gulf shipping. The US took no action against the IRGC in response. On the night of September 21, however, US Special Forces helicopters using night-vision equipment observed an Iranian amphibious landing craft dropping cylindrical objects into the Gulf. The helicopters attacked the vessel, and when US forces boarded (and scuttled) it, they discovered mines with the same markings as those found in Gulf waters; they also found Iranian government orders to engage in the mining operation.[21] When the US frigate *Samuel B. Roberts* was struck in early October by a newly laid Iranian mine, the US Navy implemented Operation Praying Mantis, commencing with the destruction of three oil platforms, and leading thereafter (when Iranian vessels responded) to the sinking of an Iranian missile boat, a frigate, and several small IRGC gunboats, as well as severely damaging an F-4 aircraft and another frigate. In *The Twilight War*, Daniel Crist provides a detailed account of these events, which he concludes convinced Iran's admirals that "they should not take on the U.S. Navy."[22] He supports the view that Iran will refrain from attacking its enemies only when IRGC aggression is confronted.[23]

The US initially suspended negotiations in The Hague when the president authorized military action against Iranian vessels and platforms after IRGC attacks on US and US-flagged vessels and the mining of Gulf waters. But negotiations were soon resumed, at Iran's request, as described below, demonstrating at least in that instance that actively defending against IRGC aggression can enhance rather than undermine the possibility of effective diplomatic engagement.

President George H.W. Bush

President Bush called for the release of US hostages seized in Lebanon in his first address to Congress in January 1989, adding, "Good will begets good will." He promised that assistance in achieving the hostages' release would long be appreciated.

Soon after the president's address, I wrote a memorandum to Secretary of State James Baker noting the importance Iran attributed to the claims process in The Hague and pointing out that settlements of the remaining claims provided an opportunity for the parties to express good will toward each other without compromising principles. The US had properly refused to bargain for the release of the hostages in Lebanon, but I recommended that the fact that hostages might be released as a result of fair settlements should not lead the US to refuse to agree to such settlements. The Administration authorized me to continue to pursue settlements of US and Iranian claims, and to cooperate with Iran in resolving disputes related to them.

President Bush strongly favored (and as vice president had approved) the payment of damages to the victims of the 1988 US shoot-down of Iran Air 655, which killed 290 civilians, including 254 Iranians. I renewed the US offer to pay damages directly to each victim, which Iran eventually accepted. My discussions in The Hague with Dr. Eftekhar resulted in numerous settlements of claims and some helpful understandings. It was awkward to have Rafsanjani continue to repeat that Iran would "definitely take reciprocal steps if assured that its assets frozen in the United States would be released."[24] But the president was undeterred by the questions these statements raised and the Administration simply (and accurately) rejected the existence of any quid pro quo between the legal work being done and the hostage problem.

The US made several practical gestures to Iran related to the claims process. These included allowing US companies to be paid what Iran owed them in oil and allowing purchases of oil from Iran where the funds involved were deposited in the security account established at the tribunal in The Hague. In October 1989, the US encouraged Ashland Oil to pay the National Iranian Oil Company some $325 million it owed for oil delivered to Ashland ten years earlier. Then, in November, the US announced that it had agreed to allow Iran to withdraw $567 million from an account that had been set up to pay US bank claims. The US supported this outcome, since the bank claims for which the reserve account was created had been resolved, and Iran agreed to place $243 million from that account into the general security account to pay other claims that might arise. Rather than waiting for the tribunal to order the US to give the funds back to Iran, which would only have delayed the transfer, I negotiated the agreement to release most of the funds without delay.

Reactions in the American press to the announced return to Iran of the $567 million focused on its possible relationship to the hostage issue. The State Department rejected any such linkage: "We are making no deals with anyone about the hostages."[25] President Bush made clear, on the other hand, that he wanted to "get this underbrush [of claims] cleaned out now" and that he would welcome the Iranians doing "what they can to influence those who hold these hostages."[26] The official Islamic Republic News Agency promptly issued a statement that the release of $567 million in frozen assets "was not enough to persuade Tehran to intervene on behalf of 18 Western hostages held in Lebanon."[27] We disregarded such statements and pushed ahead with the work. Anxiety among State Department officials continued; they were concerned that we would be accused of settling claims in exchange for the release of hostages. At one point, I asked sarcastically at a departmental meeting if they wanted me to refuse to agree to settlements unless the Iranians agreed that hostages would *not* be released.

The president had it right. Claims continued to be settled, and we continued to face and live with newspaper speculation that "these 'out of court settlements' may be paving the way towards a normalization of relations between Iran and the U.S."[28] Simultaneously, in February 1990, President Rafsanjani, the Ayatollah Mohammed Hussein Fadlallah (a leading Shiite cleric in Lebanon), and others began openly stating that the continued detention of the hostages in Lebanon was being used by the US and other Western powers to denigrate Iran and Islam.[29]

In late April of that year, US hostages Robert Polhill and Frank Reed were released. The Administration conveyed its thanks to Iran and Syria for their assistance, but in a muted form due to the continued detention of several other Americans. Within days, I was back in The Hague as previously scheduled, where Dr. Eftekhar was obviously pleased that two hostages had been freed and did not attempt to disclaim credit for the action. We then completed work on a settlement that covered more than 2,370 US and 108 Iranian small claims (of less than $250,000 each), in exchange for lump sum payments netting the US more than $104 million.[30] Questions were raised in the press about the relationship of the settlement and the release of the two hostages, and once again the State Department rejected any such relationship, noting that the settlement had been in the works for many months.

In fact, as the department consistently asserted, during my tenure in The Hague, no discussions ever took place involving an exchange of funds or settlements for the release of hostages. But at each of my meetings there, as instructed, I informed Dr. Eftekhar that, while our work in settling cases was unrelated to the continued detention of US hostages in Lebanon, good relations between Iran and the US could only be restored if the hostages were released. He invariably responded that, while Iran did not control the hostages, it would do what it could to urge their release.

All told, the claims negotiations contributed to the process by which Iran decided to help free the hostages and to seek a better relationship with the US. They demonstrated how US/Iran negotiations could be productive. In an op-ed, published in July 1990, I urged that the claims talks be continued with the same persistence with which they had been conducted under President Bush: an "open, long-term negotiating process in the face of occasional criticism and speculation that we were negotiating for the release of hostages," and I predicted that "continued progress at the same pace could result in settlements of nearly all remaining matters within the next year."[31]

Meanwhile, a more significant negotiation was underway, specifically aimed at bringing about the hostage release. President Bush's call for release of the hostages, and his promise that good will would beget good will, led UN Secretary General Perez de Cuellar to authorize a multi-year, intense effort to resolve the hostage issue. UN envoy Giandomenico Picco led this effort, with de Cuellar's support and at critical points his personal involvement. Picco sought Iran's cooperation in exchange for a variety of actions, including acknowledgment by the UNSC that Iraq had illegally started the 1980s war with Iran and the release by Israel of hundreds of Hezbollah prisoners. He explicitly assured Iran it would gain improved relations with the US if the hostages were released, and also reportedly promised Rafsanjani and others, without any specific basis, that President Bush would "react swiftly by taking action on Iranian monetary assets blocked by the United States and other appropriate gestures. . . ."[32]

Picco's prospects for success were significantly improved by an unanticipated event that followed Saddam Hussein's invasion of Kuwait. When Iraqi forces overran Kuwait City, they released the "Dawa-17," a group of Hezbollah terrorists responsible for attacking the US embassy in Kuwait. Hezbollah had made release of the Dawa-17 (one of whom was Imad Mugniyah's brother-in-law) a condition for Hezbollah's cooperation in securing the hostages' release.

It also helped that Rafsanjani, the Ayatollah Fadlallah, and others continued to state publicly that holding the hostages no longer served Iran's or Islam's interests; by April 1991, in fact, they had concluded that release of the hostages should no longer be linked to the return of Iranian assets.[33] Iran's leaders were also impressed by the Bush Administration's effectiveness in driving Iraq out of Kuwait, no doubt noting the clear superiority of US conventional forces. "As Mr. Perez de Cuellar sees it, had it not been for the Persian Gulf War, American hostages might still be in captivity."[34] A knowledgeable White House official viewed the war as " 'the single most dramatic political and military event' that led to release of the hostages. . . ."[35] Israel also helped by releasing prisoners in southern Lebanon, hoping throughout the process to obtain information about missing Israeli military personnel.[36]

On November 18, 1991, two more hostages, Terry Waite and Thomas Sutherland, were released from Lebanon. Simultaneously, the US and Iran finalized a settlement almost completed before I left the State Department that involved paying for Iran's undelivered military equipment. The two events were not linked. The settlement was signed and implemented when, after a long delay, Iran agreed to deposit $18 million of the $278 million the US agreed to pay into the Tribunal security account. The State Department correctly pointed out: "This agreement has been under discussion for a long time." On the other hand, it is not accurate to say that the settlement, as well as the claims process in general, had "nothing to do with the hostage releases." As I pointed out at the time, while we did not negotiate for the hostages in the claims discussions, we always made clear that their release was something we wanted and that had to occur before the relationship between Iran and the US could be normalized. We were not negotiating for the hostages, or paying the Iranians "more money than they deserve. It's just that [when] there's a settlement, then a better relationship [is created] and that helps release hostages."[37] All these factors, then, in addition to the critically important negotiating efforts of de Cuellar and

Picco, led in December 1991 to the release of all the remaining US and other foreign hostages in Lebanon.

Although Iran's efforts had been instrumental in securing the hostages' release, this did not result in the improved relations that President Bush had suggested would occur, which Picco had promised, and which Rafsanjani and many others in Iran expected.[38] The Administration believed that Rafsanjani had paid up to $2 million to the captors of each of the hostages released.[39] Picco was invited to the White House after the hostage releases and received a medal in appreciation for his work. But he also got some very bad news. He was told that Iran's continued support for terrorism made it impossible for the US to respond positively to its assistance.

No one could have been surprised in December 1991 that the IRGC was continuing to support terrorism and other activities that the US disapproved. The IRGC was not under Rafsanjani's control, and may in fact have been pleased to disrupt any possible improvement in US/Iranian relations. Rafsanjani himself must have supported most of the IRGC activities that led the Bush Administration to refuse to engage diplomatically with Iran, including the assassination in Paris in August 1991 of former Iranian Prime Minister Shapour Bakhtiar and other foreign assassinations of political enemies; the continued refusal to lift the *fatwa* calling for the death of author Salman Rushdie; continued interference with US efforts to settle Israeli/Palestinian disputes; indications of a desire to develop nuclear weapons technologies; assisting Hezbollah in taking revenge for the Israeli assassination of Sheikh Musawi and his family in Lebanon in February 1992; facilitating attacks against the Jewish Community Center and Israeli Embassy in Argentina; and murdering Iranian Kurds at the Mykonos Restaurant in Berlin.[40]

Picco was devastated when he learned that the US was unwilling to respond positively to Iran's assistance in securing the hostages' freedom. Having given his word that such an improvement would take place, he insisted upon reporting the news to President Rafsanjani in person, much to the chagrin of Rafsanjani's staff, who wanted to minimize rather than dramatize the fact that Rafsanjani would have nothing to show for his effort to improve relations.

High-ranking Iranian officials asked me to meet them in New York, where they expressed surprise that the US had refused to follow up on the promise of improved relations. I passed their message personally to NSC Adviser Brent Scowcroft at the White House. He confirmed that Iran's continued support for terrorist actions had made improved relations impossible. When I informed the Iranians of this response, they were shaken and deeply disappointed, having taken risks within Iran to bring about the hostage release. Iran/US relations did not improve, and the settlement process in The Hague came virtually to a halt. Rafsanjani and his supporters soon paid the price for their fruitless effort, as relative "hard-liners" increased their influence.[41]

The Bush Administration owed nothing to Iran for securing the release of hostages that Iran had likely helped terrorist groups to seize. It is also entirely appropriate that the Administration was infuriated by the IRGC's continued support of Hezbollah attacks and foreign assassinations, however expected such conduct may have become. But refusing to engage Iran after the hostage release was a weak response to the IRGC's illegal conduct and wholly ineffective at altering its behavior. Instead of reneging on a promise of negotiations that could have led to improvements in US/Iranian relations—and ultimately in IRGC conduct—the US should have responded in some tangible manner to the attacks while agreeing to negotiate. A strong response could have had some deterrent effect, could have limited the growth of IRGC influence in Iran, and would have given the Bush Administration the political credibility to test the diplomatic opening that Iran's cooperation made possible.

President William J. Clinton

The Clinton Administration initially adopted a policy of "Dual Containment" based on a hoped-for "tight web of international trade restrictions" to deprive both Iran and Iraq of access to income and technology.[42] No such "web" was achieved, but the US implemented sanctions unilaterally. In May 1993, the Administration, while disclaiming any intent to "seek a confrontation," insisted that "we will not normalize relations . . . until and unless Iran's policies change across the board."[43] Secretary of State Warren Christopher denounced Iran as an "international outlaw" and a "dangerous country"; the US used its vote to block some international loans; and the Administration announced that "the isolation of Iran should end only if Tehran halts its support for terrorism, curtails its military buildup, stops its subversion of other governments and ends its quest for nuclear weapons."[44] In March 1995, President Clinton issued Executive Order 12957 prohibiting oil deals with Iran, and in May he cut off all US trade and investment with Iran via Executive Order 12959. In December 1995, after the bombing of the Jewish Community Center in Buenos Aires and other Iranian-supported terrorist attacks, Congress adopted legislation providing $18 million to be spent on covert operations to bring about a change in Iranian conduct, a provision widely seen as approving in principle a policy of regime change. Frustrated by Iran's intransigence, President Clinton signed the legislation.[45] Iran responded by condemning US interference in its internal affairs.[46]

These policies had no impact on IRGC conduct, but they did lead the Ayatollah Khamenei to accuse those advocating a dialogue with Washington of being "simple-minded, fearful, and politically naïve."[47] In addition, the Majlis passed legislation providing $20 million to Iran's Intelligence Agency for covert efforts to offset illegal US intervention; and Iranian leaders threatened to attack the US "everywhere."[48] Within months, Iran in fact formed, trained, and supported a Saudi Hezbollah group that conducted the June 1996 assault on the Khobar Towers barracks in Saudi Arabia.[49]

The US, suspecting that Iran had supported the Khobar bombing, sought a briefing from Saudi Arabia on information obtained during its investigation. President Clinton promised to "leave no stone unturned" to find out who was responsible and ordered a plan to attack Iran that did not, in his words, rely on "piss-ant half mea-sures."[50] According to Kenneth M. Pollack, who was then on the NSC staff, the Saudis offered to provide the information, but supposedly only if the US agreed in advance to "a massive military campaign" against Iran. The US reportedly refused to agree to that arrangement, but the Saudi offer, combined with what the US knew, certainly indi-cated that Iran was responsible. Intelligence officials reportedly doubted "that there will ever be clear-cut proof. But if such proof was found, there would be extraordinary pressure on President Clin-ton to retaliate militarily, a senior White House official said."

Military commanders reportedly had "little appetite" for what they called a "symbolic strike" similar to what one of them described as having been conducted by the US Navy in 1987 and 1988. "We certainly could do something like that militarily," one said, adding, "I'm not sure what it would accomplish. Iran would almost cer-tainly respond and it could start a cycle of violence."[51] This wholly inaccurate description of the significance of Operation Praying Mantis went unanswered; as David Crist makes clear in his detailed description of the operation, the attacks of 1988, though limited, accomplished a great deal by forcing the IRGC to end its attacks on US-flagged vessels and its mining of the Gulf.[52]

Khobar Towers was not the only evidence of IRGC aggression at the time. Iran was building up its navy and was frequently harassing US public vessels in the Gulf. Notably, in October 1997, an IRGC patrol boat "made an unexpected turn, and hit" the US cruiser *Get-tysburg*. This was only one of several, less consequential encounters, which prompted concerns among US military planners about an escalation to more serious confrontations—especially since the Irani-ans had recently acquired potent Chinese anti-ship missiles.[53] Reve-lations about the IRGC were also emerging at this time in Berlin, where prosecutors were pressing criminal charges for the Mykonos Restaurant murders of Kurdish Iranians.

President Clinton nonetheless decided against military action. He wrote in his biography, after leaving office, that Iran's involvement in the bombing raised "difficult and dangerous questions," and asked rhetorically, "Even if we had a good defense against attacks, would law enforcement be a sufficient offensive strategy against terrorists? If not, would greater reliance on military options work? In the middle of 1996, it was clear that we didn't have all the answers on how to deal with attacks on Americans in the country and overseas. . . ."[54] The president provided no answer to those questions, however, apparently advancing them as his explanation for doing nothing beyond allowing the criminal investigation of Khobar Towers to proceed without Saudi input. In the absence of an executive branch response, Congress adopted the Iran/Libya Sanctions Act in July, providing for the imposition of penalties against any foreign company that had over $20 million or more invested in the Iranian or Libyan oil industries.

Any prospect that the Administration might act against the IRGC for sponsoring the Khobar assault ended in 1997, when Mohammad Khatami was elected president of Iran in a surprise victory. Khatami announced that his country considered the American people citizens of a "great nation," and suggested increased cultural and educational exchanges to open "a crack in this wall of mistrust" between the two nations. He came close to apologizing for the seizure of US diplomats during the Iranian Revolution, calling at the same time for the US to apologize for supporting the 1953 coup of President Mossadegh.[55] He said that Iran would conduct normal relations with any state that accepts "our independence," and would "shake the hand of all nations who believe in the principles of mutual respect."[56] Khatami's government also announced that, while it opposed making peace with Israel, it would not impose its views on the Palestinians. Iranian ships in the Gulf began to behave with consistent courtesy.[57]

Starting in late 1997, President Clinton responded to Khatami's statements with a series of gestures: relaxing visa restrictions, placing the anti-regime Iranian group MEK on the State Department's terrorism list, and removing Iran from the list of nations that did not cooperate adequately in the suppression of illegal narcotics. In January 1998, the president endorsed Khatami's call for people-to-people exchanges, insisting however that "government-to-government dialogue won't happen until Tehran renounces terrorism, opposition to the Middle East peace process, and weapons of mass destruction."

In June 1998, Secretary of State Madeleine Albright gave a speech describing what she called a "road map to normal relations" with Iran. She announced liberalized rules for the issuance of visas to Iranians, and called for improved cultural and educational relations. She asked Iran to take parallel steps and to stop supporting terrorism, violating the human rights of its people, undermining efforts to bring about peace between Israel and the Palestinians, and acquiring the capacity to develop nuclear weapons.

Official Iran radio noted these developments, but commented that the US had not revised its positions enough to warrant a change in relations; also, the program declared, the US must renounce support for violence against Iran by opposition groups in Iraq, return Iranian assets, and "apologize to the Iranian nation for its wrong policies in the past 50 years."[58] In September, Iran's Foreign Minister, Kamal Kharrazi, responded formally to Secretary Albright's June proposals, noting the "new tone" but rejecting her speech as an inadequate "variation in verbiage" with no concrete incentives. He said the US lacked a commitment to international law and was retarding Iran's economy by blocking a planned pipeline and imposing sanctions. He also protested the covert program approved by Congress to destabilize the Iranian government by waging a propaganda war through a Persian-language radio station. He condemned Albright for defending US support of the Shah as an "attempt to justify the wrongful past," and blamed the US for the 1953 coup that led to the Shah's rule.[59]

On June 18, 1998, President Clinton, apparently responding to the Khatami Administration's demand for an apology, made some after-dinner remarks at the White House in which he acknowledged that strained relations were the result of US as well as Iranian mistakes. He said that Iran was changing in positive ways and that the US sought "a genuine reconciliation" in which Iranians were prepared "to move away from support of terrorism and distribution of dangerous weapons," and to end Tehran's opposition to the Middle East peace process.[60] He did not mention Iran's role in the Khobar Towers bombing. Soon thereafter, the US modified sanctions on Iran to exclude food and medicines.[61]

Meanwhile, FBI Director Freeh was pressing the Administration to get Saudi Arabia to share the evidence it had accumulated from several individuals arrested for the Khobar Towers bombing. He had asked repeatedly that President Clinton seek Saudi cooperation, but no progress was made. In 1998, when Freeh heard that former President Bush was going on a visit to Saudi Arabia, he asked the former president to intervene with the Saudis. The president did so and reported that the Saudis had readily agreed to cooperate; he also said the Saudis had told him that Clinton officials had never specifically asked for cooperation.

After President Bush's intervention, FBI agents were given access to witnesses in Saudi Arabia who provided information that established to their satisfaction that Iran was responsible for the bombing. Freeh later wrote that, when he presented National Security Adviser Sandy Berger this information, Berger reacted negatively ("Who knows about this?"), claiming the information was "just hearsay" (despite the established exception for co-conspirator statements). Freeh concluded that Berger seemed more interested in preventing dissemination of the evidence than in using it even to indict the culprits, let alone as a basis for holding the IRGC accountable for sponsoring the bombing.[62]

The record establishes, therefore, that President Clinton and his Administration were aware before 1999 that the IRGC had supported if not planned the Khobar Towers bombing.[63] But the Administration was eager to continue trying to achieve better relations with Iran while President Khatami was still in power, and apparently feared that an attack on those responsible for the bombing (the

IRGC) would prevent progress. Khatami at that time continued to pursue a soft line, disavowing terrorism and claiming that Islam was a religion of love and tolerance. The US reciprocated with additional gestures, approving in December 1999, for example, Boeing's sale to Iran of safety-related spare parts for civilian airliners.

In February 2000, Khatami's party won over 70 percent of the seats in the Iranian parliament. The Clinton Administration became even more determined to continue its appeals to Khatami for a better relationship rather than to deal with the IRGC's responsibility for the Khobar bombing and other criminal acts. The Administration announced soon after Khatami's victory that it was "looking at ways to engage Iran in a dialogue and to recognize the important changes that are taking place there."[64] Foreign Minister Kharrazi called for the lifting of economic sanctions, which he said would be "a big victory" for Iran; his government insisted, however, that talks would be held only if the US treated Iran with respect and "releases Iranian assets, valued at $12 billion, frozen in American banks since the Islamic revolution."[65]

In March 2000, in a speech at the Asia Society, Secretary Albright added to the concessions made in her 1997 speech.[66] In an effort "to broaden our perspective," she acknowledged US failings in its dealings with Iran, specifically America's "significant role in orchestrating the 1953 overthrow of Iran's popular Prime Minister, Mohammed Mossadegh"; its "sustained backing" for the Shah's regime, which, while improving the economy, "brutally repressed political dissent"; and its "regrettably shortsighted" support of Saddam Hussein. "As President Clinton has said," she continued, "the United States must bear its fair share of responsibility for the problems that have arisen in U.S.-Iranian relations." Yet Iran, too, had behaved improperly, Secretary Albright insisted, by pursuing its nuclear program and supporting terrorism; and she noted that "control over the military, judiciary, courts, and police remains in unelected hands." But, she concluded, "the question both countries now face is whether to allow the past to freeze the future or to find a way to plant the seeds of a new relationship that will enable us to harvest shared advantages in years to come, not more tragedies."

To encourage a positive response, Albright announced significant US gestures: adjustments in economic sanctions to allow the import of Iranian rugs and food products; willingness to "explore ways to remove unnecessary impediments to increase contact between American and Iranian scholars, professionals, artists, athletes, and nongovernmental organizations"; and stepped up "efforts with Iran aimed at eventually concluding a global settlement of [the few but very substantial] outstanding legal claims between our two countries." She invited whatever process Iran wanted that would move the countries "to enter a new season in which mutual trust may grow and a quality of warmth supplant the long, cold winter of our mutual discontent."

Hadi Nejad-Hosseinian, Iran's ambassador to the UN, said in response that Iran would be "prepared to adopt proportionate and positive measures in return."[67] But ten days later, the Grand Ayatollah Khamenei, one of the "unelected hands" Albright had mentioned, dismissed her speech as "just another ploy . . . laying the groundwork for their sinister plots."[68] In a statement issued a few months later, he declared that any negotiations with Washington would be "an insult and treason to the Iranian people."[69] President Khatami later echoed these sentiments, stating at the UN in September that relations would not improve between Iran and the US without an "apology" that specifically included the "various sanctions," the "animosities," and the "allegations against Iran."[70] The Council on Foreign Relations publication "Timeline" on US-Iran Contacts describes Albright's speech as an "apology,"[71] but it had not gone far enough to satisfy President Khatami. Although President Clinton pointedly sat through Khatami's UN speech, an unprecedented gesture, Khatami appears to have deliberately avoided any personal contact with him.

Meanwhile, it became impossible for the Administration to ignore the evidence that the IRGC had sponsored the Khobar Towers bombing. In addition to the information obtained through Saudi cooperation, the US according to Freeh had "learned that senior members of the Iranian government, including Ministry of Defense, Ministry of Intelligence and Security (MOIS), and the Spiritual Leader's office had selected Khobar as their target and commissioned the Saudi Hezbollah to carry out the operation."[72] Determined to avoid upsetting the Iranians, however, the Administration arranged a secret meeting with Iranians in Oman, informed them that the US had "credible" evidence of Iran's responsibility for Khobar Towers, and asked that those responsible be prosecuted.[73] The Administration also sent a letter to Khatami, through Oman, citing the cooperation received from Saudi Arabia and calling on him to prosecute the IRGC leaders involved and to stop supporting terrorism. The letter reached the Ayatollah Khamenei, however, exposing the Saudis and leading to a public denunciation from Iran that it was the Americans who were the terrorists.[74]

By November 2000, President Clinton recognized the failure of his efforts to establish a better relationship with Iran through public appeals and unilateral concessions. He renewed US sanctions. President Khatami condemned the action, warning that the sanctions "will force us more and more to look elsewhere for what we need."[75] Even at that point, however, the Administration did nothing further in response to the IRGC's responsibility for Khobar. Although FBI Director Freeh urged that Iran be held accountable, the Administration took no action calculated to deter the IRGC from sponsoring further attacks; US officials did not even issue a public statement condemning Iran for Khobar.

In June 2001, after Freeh had retired and George W. Bush had become president, the US issued an indictment against several individuals for the Khobar bombing. It included a statement attributing the bombing to Iranian officials. No additional action was taken against the IRGC, however, and Freeh later condemned the Clinton Administration for doing nothing on the issue because its leaders were set on improving relations with what they perceived to be a moderate Iranian president. Freeh found the Administration's inaction consistent with US policy going back to 1983:

> Sadly, this fits into a larger pattern of U.S. governments sending the wrong message to Tehran. Almost 13 years before Iran committed its terrorist act of war against America at Khobar, it used its surrogates, the Lebanese Hezbollah, to murder 241 Marines in their Beirut barracks. The U.S. response to that 1983 outrage was to pull our military forces out of the region. Such timidity was not lost upon Tehran. As with Beirut, Tehran once again received loud and clear from the U.S. its consistent message that there would be no price to pay for its acts of war against America.[76]

Ironically, the Administration's failure to act against the IRGC in response to Khobar may have constituted a lost opportunity to undermine the IRGC's influence and power. Attacking the IRGC might have helped Khatami fight off the IRGC's determined efforts, with the Ayatollah Khamenei's support, to prevent Khatami's reforms from affecting Iran's international relations and Islamic control; instead, the influence of the IRGC grew, and it was able soon thereafter to help drive Khatami from power.[77]

President George W. Bush

President George W. Bush's Administration approved the Khobar Towers indictment in June 2001, explicitly alleging that Iran had directed and supported the bombing. The indictment noted that the conspirators had stated: "the purpose of the attack was to strike the United States on behalf of Iran."[78] It did not name any individual Iranians, however, and the Administration did nothing further to respond to the crime. The Administration also continued the policy of imposing sanctions on Iran, initially unilateral (including renewal of the Iran/Libya Sanctions Act limiting oil industry–

related investments), but gradually securing and expanding multi-lateral sanctions as the US won UNSC support.

The 9/11 attacks led President Bush (nine days later) to announce that the US would consider all states that sponsor terrorist attacks to be "hostile." He ordered American troops into Afghanistan soon thereafter, attacking al-Qaeda's bases and driving the Taliban from power. This strong action appears to have led Iran to seek better relations with the US. Iranian officials condemned the 9/11 attacks. President Khatami stated: "I hope that this bitter event will be the last we will have, and that terrorism and hate will be replaced by coexistence, empathy, logic, and dialogue."[79] In the following months, Iran worked cooperatively with the US on issues related to Afghanistan.

In November 2001, Secretary of State Colin Powell and Iranian Foreign Minister Kamal Kharrazi met in New York during the 6+2 Foreign Ministers' meeting on matters related to Afghanistan. Hillary Mann, then director of Iran, Afghanistan, and Persian Gulf Affairs at the National Security Council, has written that Iran's help was critical to the "adoption of [the] ministerial statement of principles that committed the parties to combat terrorism."[80] Iranian officials agreed to set up a "post-Taliban political order," after pledging to use "whatever statistics regarding the ethnic and sectarian composition of Afghanistan's population that the U.S. government preferred."[81]

Following the Bonn conference of December 2001, Mann and other US officials held monthly meetings with their Iranian counter-parts in Europe, and Ambassador James Dobbins, US envoy to Afghanistan, met with Iranians regarding the situation in that country. Secretary Powell said of the secret talks taking place in Europe in December 2001: "I am open to explore opportunities. We have been in discussions with the Iranians on a variety of levels and in some new ways since September 11. . . . [W]e are open to exploring opportunities without having Vaseline in our eyes with respect to the nature of the government or the history of the past 22 years."[82]

In January 2002, Iranian diplomats told Dobbins that Iran would like to "open a broad dialogue with the U.S."[83] The countries seemed poised to engage more meaningfully than in the past.

On November 8, 2001, however, the CIA began reporting to the president that the IRGC was providing weapons to the Taliban in Afghanistan and allowing al-Qaeda operatives there to escape capture by leaving through Iran.[84] On January 3, 2002, in the Red Sea, Israel intercepted the *Karine A*, loaded with weapons made in and shipped from Iran to the Palestinian Authority. Their purpose: to convert the Palestinian intifada into a military confrontation similar to what Israel faced with Hezbollah in Lebanon. The interception, coming at a time when the US was trying to broker a ceasefire between Palestinians and Israelis, made clear that Iran was continuing to support terrorist activities, and that it remained intent on disrupting the peace process and attacking Israel. Secretary of Defense Donald Rumsfeld noted at the time, moreover, the accumulation of evidence that Iran had cooperated with al-Qaeda prior to 9/11: "We have any number of reports that Iran has been permissive and allowed transit through their country of al-Qaeda."[85]

Discoveries that Iran was continuing to support terrorism and undermine the Middle East peace process led President Bush in his 2002 State of the Union address to brand Iran and its "terrorist allies" as part of "an axis of evil, arming to threaten the peace of the world." On January 31, 2002, National Security Adviser Condoleezza Rice said: "Iran's direct support of regional and global terrorism, and its aggressive efforts to acquire weapons of mass destruction, belie any good intentions it displayed in the days after the world's worst terrorist attacks in history."[86]

Iran responded by openly resuming and arguably escalating its anti-US activities. Foreign Minister Kharrazi said of President Bush's speech: "It is very strange for us, and shocked everyone, why Americans after all this cooperation in Afghanistan came up with this notion of the 'axis of evil.'"[87] Soon thereafter, Iran released Taliban commander Gulbuddin Hekmatyar, enabling him to return to

Afghanistan to become a major cause of instability and danger to NATO forces.[88] Iran also began actively assisting Shiites in Iraq in their fight against the US and Coalition forces, and it gave al-Qaeda members refuge in Iran; one of them planned the May 2003 bombing of a Western housing complex in Riyadh, Saudi Arabia, which killed thirty-five people, including nine Americans.

Meanwhile, Ambassador Dobbins and other senior US officials continued to meet with Iranian diplomats. Talks initially focused on Afghanistan but later switched to other issues, such as al-Qaeda fugitives and later still, the Iraq war.[89] The US and other coalition forces toppled the Iraqi regime in early April 2003, and once again in the wake of a powerful demonstration of US strength, the Iranian government sought better relations. During April, former President Rafsanjani publicly called for restoring ties with the US, as did a majority of the Majlis; polls indicated that more than 70 percent of Iranians favored such a move.[90] In early May, the Swiss Ambassador to Iran, Tim Guldimann, who represented US interests there, produced a letter he claimed Iranian officials had given him proposing a "grand bargain" that would address a number of US concerns, including nuclear weapons, support of Hamas and Hezbollah, and a two-state solution to the Israeli-Palestinian conflict.[91] In return, the US was to lift sanctions, end "hostile behavior" toward Iran, and accept the latter's right to develop a peaceful nuclear program.[92]

Bush Administration officials were divided on the significance of the alleged message; ultimately, the US government criticized the Swiss government for "'overstepping' its mandate by transmitting the message," and decided against making a response.[93] Several commentators supported the view of Sadegh Kharrazi, Iran's Ambassador to France and co-author of the proposal, that the Administration had missed a "golden opportunity"; Deputy Secretary of State Richard Armitage noted, on the other hand: "We could not determine what [in the proposal] was the Iranians' and what was the Swiss ambassador's."[94]

The May 2003 bombings in Riyadh halted all discussions between the US and Iran for more than two years. In late 2003, however, negotiations commenced between Iran and three European countries (France, Germany, and the United Kingdom), with the Europeans agreeing to discuss a range of nuclear, security, and economic issues if Iran suspended uranium enrichment. In early 2004, IAEA inspectors found in Iran an undisclosed design for advanced centrifuges. Perhaps embarrassed by this disclosure, Iranian officials agreed soon thereafter to suspend "enrichment." Iran construed the term narrowly, however, and continued work on converting uranium to a form susceptible to enrichment. The Europeans rejected Iran's interpretation, and negotiations did not proceed.

In November 2004, Iran agreed to suspend all forms of enrichment, including conversion of uranium, and negotiations began. The US was skeptical that any progress could be achieved, since Iran's negotiator, Hassan Rowhani, publicly insisted that Iran would never surrender its "right" to enrichment; he secured a written provision in the agreement that suspension was a "voluntary confidence-building measure and not a legal obligation." Despite these statements, and his promise (rejected by the Europeans) that the suspension would last only "months, not years," Rowhani and his team were attacked in Iran for making concessions, one journalist accusing him of giving up a "pearl in exchange for a lollipop."[95] The parties traded detailed proposals, but made no progress; the US refused to join the process, on occasion issuing threats and implying "that Iran may be the next Iraq."[96]

The US did not venture beyond threats, however, despite extensive and damaging IRGC assistance to coalition enemies in Iraq and other illegal actions. In the nuclear negotiations, Iran, in August 2005, rejected the European approach and resumed its nuclear activities, because the Europeans refused to recognize Iran's right to enrichment. Russia tried to help by proposing in October that Iran share ownership of a uranium-enrichment plant in Russia, but Iran rejected that proposal in March of the following year.[97]

In July 2005, US Ambassador to Afghanistan, Ronald Neumann, was allowed to meet with the Iranian ambassador there, but discussions between them were limited to Afghanistan-related issues; no conversation about "overall US-Iranian relations or other subjects" was permitted.[98] Soon thereafter, Neumann was told to stop having any meetings with Iranian officials. He later explained why he considered that decision mistaken:

> The decision to stop holding meetings was a part of Washington's broader policy to press Iran in all channels on the nuclear issue. On two or three occasions I recommended verbally to then Secretary of State Rice that I be authorized to resume the discussions about Afghanistan with Iran, but the policy of suspension remained in force as of the time of my departure in April 2007.[99]

In early 2006, Iran unsuccessfully attempted to begin backchannel talks with Stephen Hadley, then US national security advisor.[100] In May, however, Secretary Rice began implementing a new policy that offered multinational negotiations if the five other nations already involved agreed to demand that Iran freeze nuclear enrichment activities as a precondition to negotiations, to support UNSC resolutions that required Iran to accept the group's demands, and to impose sanctions on Iran if it failed to comply.[101] In June, China, Russia, and the US joined the EU3 (P5+1) and offered a comprehensive proposal in which, in exchange for agreeing to suspend enrichment-related and reprocessing activities and resuming adherence to the Additional Protocol of the NPT, Iran would receive state-of-the-art light-water reactors, nuclear fuel guarantees, and a five-year buffer stock of fuel, a suspension of UNSC discussion of Iran's nuclear program, and cooperation between the EU, US, and Iran on civil aviation, telecommunications, high technology, agriculture, and other areas of commerce. "If Iran were looking for a path toward normalizing relations with the United States," Secretary Rice announced, "nuclear negotiations could be the starting point."[102]

In July, acting pursuant to the P5+1's understandings, the UNSC adopted Resolution 1696 endorsing the proposal advanced by the P5+1, calling on Iran to comply with IAEA demands and on all other states to prevent the transfer of any items "that could contribute to Iran's enrichment-related and reprocessing activities and ballistic missile programs." If Iran had not complied with the resolution by August 31, the resolution warned, the council would adopt appropriate measures "under Article 41 of Chapter VII of the" UN Charter.

On August 22, Iran responded to the P5+1 proposal with a 21-page counterproposal rejecting the precondition that it suspend uranium enrichment but agreeing to negotiations and noting that the P5+1 document contained "useful foundations and capacities for comprehensive and long-term cooperation between the two sides."[103] Russia and China viewed Iran's response as a basis for further discussions, but France, Germany, and the US said the response "falls short" of the demand that Iran suspend uranium enrichment by August 31.[104] In September, the US imposed financial sanctions on Iranian banks. The P5+1 rejected out of hand Iran's verbal renewal of a proposal that France monitor Iran's uranium enrichment activities.[105]

The Iraq Study Group (chaired by former Secretary of State James A. Baker III and former Representative Lee H. Hamilton) urged the Bush Administration to engage more actively in negotiations with Syria, and with less emphasis to engage Iran. The recommendation related to Iran was only one element of the study group's report's seventy-nine recommendations; they addressed many other issues, including the war in Iraq, the Middle East peace process, and the desirability of coaxing Syria away from Iran. President Bush did not accept the proposal to engage directly with Iran, repeating his Administration's view that Iran had to give up its nuclear program as a precondition for talks with the US: "If they want to sit down at the table with the United States, it's easy—just make some decisions that will lead to peace, not to conflict."[106]

Nevertheless, the Administration continued to participate in the P5+1 process, and that began to result in fundamental UNSC declarations regarding international obligations and some multilateral sanctions. On December 23, the UNSC adopted Resolution 1737; acting under Article 41 of Chapter VII, the council ordered Iran to comply with "steps required by the IAEA" and without further delay to suspend "all enrichment-related and reprocessing activities" as well as "work on all heavy water–related projects," including construction of a research reactor.[107] The resolution ordered all states to prevent the supply to Iran of many types of equipment and technological assistance related to both its nuclear program and to "the development of nuclear weapon delivery systems," and it imposed a freeze of assets and other financial sanctions on designated persons and entities involved in the nuclear program to be administered by a Security Council task force. This resolution did not lead to any increased willingness on Iran's part to accept the mandated limitations; so, on March 24, 2007, the council adopted Resolution 1747, which reaffirmed existing limitations and imposed new ones on the transfer to Iran of certain types of conventional arms. The resolution also added, to the sanctions the council had previously imposed, a prohibition on dealing with many individuals and entities as well as a description of the long-term agreement proposed in 2006, which it noted remained on the table.

Still, no progress was made, and President Ahmadinejad said that no room existed for agreement even as Iran's negotiators continued to hold meetings with European diplomats. President Bush and Vice President Dick Cheney expressed their impatience in threatening terms, declaring that the US "will not allow" Iran to obtain nuclear weapons and that "our country, and the entire international community, cannot stand by as a terror-supporting state fulfills its most aggressive ambitions."[108] Despite such repeated condemnations, the US continued doing nothing in response to IRGC-supported terrorism in many places and its supply of armor-penetrating explosives to Iran's allies in Iraq, enabling them to kill many American soldiers.

A final effort to achieve progress in negotiations with Iran during the Bush Administration was made in March 2008, when the P5+1 advanced ideas that built on the 2006 proposal. It added commitments to treat Iran as a regular member of the NPT regime once confidence was restored in the nature of Iran's nuclear program, to provide technical and financial assistance for that program, to avoid any threat or use of force, to support Iran's economic integration and WTO membership, and to cooperate on Afghanistan and on other economic, social, environmental, and humanitarian issues.

Simultaneously, on March 3, the UNSC adopted Resolution 1803, repeating prior requirements, noting that the P5+1 had made enhanced diplomatic efforts in their new proposal, blocking the travel of individuals associated with prohibited activities, and restricting the use of major Iranian financial institutions to prevent their contributing to proliferation of nuclear weapons or delivery systems. The US did not participate in a June 2008 meeting to discuss this proposal, but did participate in a meeting on the subject the following month in Geneva. Iran proposed a process for negotiations, but it included no reference to its nuclear program, and no progress was made.

In conclusion, it is clear that the Bush Administration responded with strength to major, unprecedented challenges in Afghanistan and Iraq. By joining with the other members of the P5+1 and Germany in negotiating with Iran, the Administration obtained UNSC resolutions ordering Iran to cooperate with the IAEA and to stop enrichment activities, and imposing sanctions if it failed to do so. At no point in its eight years in office, however, did the Administration take overt military action against the IRGC for any of its illegal actions. This failure to respond with anything more than threats and the imposition of sanctions brought no reduction in IRGC-sponsored terrorism and attacks on the US; if anything, the IRGC escalated its illegal activities. Nor did the Administration's strategy

lead Iran to cease or even slow its nuclear program; again, if anything, the program received a higher priority, and Iranian leaders
increased enrichment activities and missile development.

Refusing to negotiate, despite the advice of experienced American
diplomats that the US should respond to Iran's requests to engage,
likewise proved ineffective. Had the Administration responded to
IRGC aggression by acting firmly against the organization's assets,
rather than by issuing empty threats, it may have been politically
able to conduct effective negotiations with Iran and to bring about
improved understandings and cooperation.

President Barack Obama

Despite the scorn with which Iran had rejected Reagan and Clinton
Administration overtures, President Barack Obama, in March 2009,
issued his own on the Iranian New Year (Nowruz) with a greeting
in Farsi, and praise for the medieval poet Saadi. He urged the Islamic
Republic of Iran to "take its rightful place in the community of
nations." This "right," he said, "comes with real responsibilities, and
that place cannot be reached through terror or arms, but rather
through peaceful actions that demonstrate the true greatness of
the Iranian people and civilization." Calling for a "new begin-
ning," the president made no reference to any aspect of Iran's conduct that the US had tried for years to alter, including its nuclear
program and support for terrorism. By indicating a willingness to
accept the Islamic regime, the speech contrasted sharply with those
made during the Bush Administration.

The president's appeal was promptly brushed aside by Grand
Ayatollah Ali Khamenei as a "slogan of change, but in practice no
change is seen."[109] An adviser to President Ahmadinejad said that
the US would have to "recognize its past mistakes and repair them
as a way to put away the differences," including repealing the unjust
sanctions.[110]

Following this exchange, Iran was invited to participate in a conference on Afghanistan at The Hague. A brief meeting between US envoy Richard Holbrooke and Deputy Foreign Minister Mahdi Akhundzadeh was cordial, and the governments continued to seek cooperation on issues related to that war-torn country. President Obama sent a second letter to the Ayatollah Khamenei requesting further cooperation between the two nations and increased dialogue.[111] Khamenei responded: "They say 'we have extended a hand towards Iran.' If the extended hand is covered with a velvet glove but underneath it, the hand is made of cast iron, this does not have a good meaning at all."[112]

An opportunity for progress on nuclear issues presented itself in June 2009, when Iran advised the IAEA that it was seeking fuel for its Tehran Research Reactor, US-supplied equipment that produces medical isotopes. The US proposed that it send 120 kilos of fuel for the TRR in exchange for Iran shipping out an equivalent amount of 4 percent-enriched uranium, or about 1200 kilos, which at that time constituted 80 percent of the country's low-enrichment uranium (LEU) stockpile. Iranian negotiators responded positively to this proposal, and in Geneva in October, Undersecretary of State for Political Affairs William Burns and National Council Secretary Saeed Jalili agreed in principle on the deal.[113] But the deal ultimately failed to secure final approval because of strong opposition within Iran, leading to proposals that it be modified to provide for the transfer out of Iran of lesser amounts of LEU than had been specified. That change was rejected by the P5+1, so Iran began increasing the level of its own enrichment activities to 20 percent in February 2010, ostensibly for TRR fuel.[114] Before long, Brazil and Turkey joined Iran in an attempt to preserve the fuel-swap idea; they issued a declaration that all three states had rights under the NPT to research, produce, and use nuclear energy and to engage in the entire fuel cycle, including enrichment. Under this arrangement, Iran would ship 1,200 kilos of LEU to Turkey in escrow; the P5+1 would approve this collaboration and within one year would transfer 120 kilos of 20-percent-enriched uranium to Iran, or Turkey would return the LEU to Iran. The P5+1 said no because the deal was silent on Iran's continued enrichment of fuel to 20 percent, an omission that potentially allowed such enrichment regardless of the fuel-swap arrangement.

In the midst of these discussions, US intelligence discovered that Iran had built the Fordow facility, underground near Qom, at a former IRGC base. Iran disclosed the site formally to the IAEA in September 2009, claiming that the new operation would eventually house 3,000 centrifuges enriching uranium up to 5 percent; later that month, Iranian officials said they would be moving their 20 percent enrichment facility from Natanz to Fordow. Although the US protested Iran's late disclosure, enrichment began in January 2010, well before the 180-day notice period that, according to Iran, applied to this situation.

The UNSC reacted by adopting Resolution 1929 in June. The resolution declared that Iran had failed to satisfy IAEA requirements and declared that Iran: must promptly ratify the Additional Protocol; could not begin new, and must cease ongoing, construction of any new uranium-enrichment, reprocessing, or heavy water–related facility; could not invest in such facilities in any other state; and "shall not undertake any activity related to ballistic missiles capable of delivering nuclear weapons." In addition, the resolution renewed and extended limitations on sales and services of both conventional arms and nuclear-related equipment to Iran and to a long list of Iranian entities, adding ships and banks to the list, and called for vigilance in dealing with the IRGC. Extending a bit of a peace feeler, the resolution confirmed that the P5+1's June 2008 proposal remained on the table, and listed at length the elements of a comprehensive arrangement that Iran could still in principle obtain if it complied with UNSC requirements.

In July 2010, President Obama signed into law the Comprehensive Iran Sanctions, Accountability, and Divestment Act, imposing penalties on companies or individuals that conduct business with

Iran's petroleum sector.[115] The continuing lack of progress in negotiations also led European countries to embrace sanctions more enthusiastically and to adopt President Sarkozy's proposed embargo on the purchase of Iranian oil, which was implemented where possible on July 1, 2012. Yet neither this measure, nor enhanced financial sanctions, have led Iran to respond positively to P5+1 proposals, and thus far the IAEA has been denied access to sites Iran is suspected of having cleaned up to remove evidence of explosives testing and other activities reflecting nuclear-weapons intentions.

President Obama has gone beyond his unsuccessful, direct appeal to Iran for a new relationship, expanding Bush Administration efforts to secure Iranian cooperation and compliance through economic and political sanctions. The strongest such efforts have only recently been put into effect. The new sanctions, however, are unlikely to be any more successful than those imposed over the last decade.

While the Obama Administration has been more willing to engage Iran directly than the George W. Bush Administration, it has been no more willing to react firmly to IRGC aggression. Obama Administration officials repeatedly accused Iran of supporting attacks on US soldiers in Iraq and Afghanistan, and even of helping al-Qaeda funnel significant amounts of money and numbers of operatives through Iran to both countries.[116] But the Administration has taken no action against the IRGC for this conduct. Secretary Panetta announced in July 2011, regarding IRGC activities in Iraq: "the solution, for now, was to pursue the weapons and militants inside Iraq, rather than to confront Iran directly."[117] In October, the Administration charged IRGC personnel with plotting to murder the Saudi ambassador, but took no military action against those involved in an attempted attack that would have killed many Americans on US soil.[118] The Administration's willingness to engage with Iran, however sincere, has been insufficient in itself to deter the IRGC or to alter Iran's diplomatic agenda.[119]

* * *

In conclusion, the record of US dealings with Iran since the Islamic Revolution makes clear that US administrations since that of President Carter have failed to defend the nation, its interests, and its allies against IRGC aggression. Instead of countering the IRGC in a manner likely to deter such conduct, the US has in virtually every instance resorted to empty threats, sanctions, and efforts to isolate Iran by refusing to negotiate with its leadership, even when negotiating may have served US interests. Direct appeals to Iran's leaders, without meaningful pressure, have proved equally futile. In the one context in which the US defended itself, in the Persian Gulf in 1987 and 1988, the response—though limited and proportionate—was effective in deterring the IRGC in the Gulf, and did not disrupt negotiations then being pursued in The Hague. Clearly the American policy of failing to respond in self-defense must end if engagement is to have any prospect of success.

CHAPTER 4

Defending Against IRGC Attacks

T he most important objective of any effort to diffuse the Iranian threat is to keep Iran from becoming a nuclear-armed state. But the United States' virtually exclusive focus on that objective has proved ineffective. Iran has been undeterred by sanctions, criminal prosecutions, and UNSC resolutions in pursuing its nuclear aims. Furthermore, preventive attacks on Iran's nuclear program are unlikely to be undertaken, if at all, until Iran has moved definitively to develop nuclear weapons (if it ever does). Expanding the available strategic options for dealing with the Iranian threat to include responding to IRGC aggression would be a lawful, legitimate, and effective way of increasing the pressure on Iran to abide by its international obligations.

Responding to IRGC aggression would constitute a useful end in itself, in that the United States has a substantial interest in deterring such IRGC activities. Implementing such a policy would increase US credibility and enhance the likelihood of Iran taking seriously the possibility of continuing US pressure in face of Iran's refusal to accept a negotiated solution to the current nuclear standoff. Moreover, US actions in self-defense are far less likely than an unprovoked preventive attack on Iran's nuclear program to lead Iran to escalate IRGC aggression or speed up its development of nuclear weapons. To the contrary, defending against the IRGC may undermine its credibility and influence, and help convince Iran to negoti-ate in earnest rather than continuing to use the negotiating process to delay additional international efforts to curb its nuclear objectives.

Legality of Defending Against IRGC Aggression

An attack by the United States on Iran's nuclear program would accurately be characterized as "preventive" rather than "defensive" until that program poses at least an "imminent" threat.[1] The United States cannot convincingly argue that Iran's nuclear program poses an imminent threat until Iran is very close to possessing or actu-ally possesses a nuclear weapon. The US can even now convincingly argue, however, that international law does permit the use of force to counter the IRGC's support of groups with which the United States is in armed conflict; to discourage the IRGC's support of surrogate or terrorist attacks that harm US nationals or violate US rights; to curb IRGC interference with international navigational rights; and to act in collective self-defense against the IRGC with other states.[2]

Acting within the parameters of established international law has tangible, as well as moral, advantages that stem ultimately from the increased support such conduct is likely to secure from the interna-tional community. It is appropriate that the United States accept the relevance of international legal limits in shaping its own conduct, when it is demanding that Iran comply with international legal requirements.

Armed Conflict Iran loses its neutrality under international law when it knowingly supplies arms and training through the IRGC to a party in any armed conflict. The Laws of Armed Conflict recog-nize this: "It is universally admitted that a neutral State cannot, without compromising its neutrality, lend aid to either belligerent (engaged in an armed conflict). . . ."[3] Iran has not even pretended to be neutral in its support of Sadrists and others in Iraq, of anti-UN forces in Afghanistan, of armed attacks by Hezbollah, and of Hamas and other groups attacking Israel.

Terrorism UNSC Resolution 1373, adopted unanimously after the 9/11 attacks, prohibits IRGC support of groups for the purpose of enabling them to attack other states. That resolution includes provisions that nations "refrain from providing any form of support, active or passive, to entities or persons involved in terrorist acts"; "prevent the commission of terrorist acts"; and "deny safe haven" to all who engage in or finance them. Resolution 1373 does not expressly authorize the use of force to deter violations of its provisions. It was, however, adopted pursuant to Chapter VII of the UN Charter, which deals with the use of force to preserve international peace and security, and contemporaneously with Resolution 1368, which expressly found that the 9/11 attacks entitled the United States to exercise its right of self-defense. While opinions of the ICJ have taken a narrower view of what constitutes an "attack" for purposes of self-defense,[4] the Security Council is the ultimate authority on state responsibility for assisting non-state actors in attacking other states. States are considered by UN doctrine to be responsible for third-party attacks only when they intend that their support be used by the groups in terrorist attacks. This standard should not be difficult to satisfy regarding the IRGC's activities, given the many statements Iranian officials have made about the happiness they derive from supplying weapons to be used to attack the US, Israel, and other enemies.[5]

The United States has consistently and repeatedly taken the position that its inherent right of self-defense entitles it to use force in situations where the use of force has traditionally been considered reasonable. For example, the United States attacked Libya in 1986 based on its expressed view that Libya was responsible and could be attacked in self-defense when it uses terrorists to attack US nationals.[6]

Navigational Rights   US-flagged vessels, including warships, have the right under international law of unimpeded transit through the Straits of Hormuz and within the Persian Gulf. The United States is entitled, therefore, to have its warships and other public vessels sail the Straits of Hormuz or other territorial seas of Iran, despite Iranian threats or orders that US warships depart the area. Secretary Panetta has made clear that the United States will not tolerate interference with the exercise of its navigational rights in the Gulf, and thus far Iran has failed to follow through on its threats to prevent that. War games have established that the IRGC could, in a surprise attack, inflict substantial damage with its hundreds of armed speedboats, advanced mines, shore-to-ship missiles, submarines, and other military resources.[7] Nonetheless, the IRGC is unlikely to confront the US Navy directly. If it does, the United States will be entitled to defend itself and seems resolved to do so.[8]

Far more difficult to deal with effectively is the harassment by IRGC speedboats of US naval vessels operating lawfully in the Gulf.[9] All vessels, including those of the IRGC, have the right of free passage in international waterways; the United States has no authority to set particular geographic limits on the approach of other ships in such waters.[10] Consistent with this rule, the United States encourages its warships to comply voluntarily with routing measures approved by the International Maritime Organization.[11] Those regulations establish rights of way, but they require vessels to avoid collisions even if that means taking actions inconsistent with the routing regulations.[12]

This presumption of safety and collision avoidance is consistent with the Standing Rules of Engagement of the US Joint Chiefs of Staff (SROEs), which provide for response to "crises" with options that (1) "are proportional to the provocation," (2) "are designed to limit the scope and intensity of the conflict," (3) "discourage escalation," and (4) "achieve political and military objectives." In the absence of an armed conflict or actual attack, these options strongly suggest avoidance of conflict (and collision) as the predominant US objectives.[13]

The United States policy favoring peaceful resolution of crises that arise in international waters is sound. US Navy commanders, however, need to be authorized to exercise their lawful discretion under international law when confronted by ships that deliberately obstruct their proper passage and behave aggressively. Such conduct includes, for example: charging US warships head-on, conducting mock attacks, transmitting verbal threats and gestures, deliberately attempting to overcome efforts to avoid collisions or close encounters. When their vessels can engage in threatening maneuvers, IRGC or IRGC-sponsored suicide bombers can attack US warships suddenly, with potentially catastrophic consequences.

No vessel has the right to behave in international waters in a manner that creates a reasonable fear of harm. The US Supreme Court has observed that "Every vessel undoubtedly has a right to the use of so much of the ocean as she occupies, and as is essential to her own movements," and "is at full liberty to pursue her voyage in her own way, and to use all necessary precautions to avoid any suspected sinister enterprise or hostile attack."[14] Naval commanders in the Gulf are ultimately responsible for the safety of their ships, and are expressly obliged by the SROEs to exercise what is ambiguously termed "the inherent **right obligation** of self-defense" (emphasis added), and to use lawful force to achieve the missions they are assigned.[15] US commanders should be given clear guidance as to the circumstances in which they will be expected to warn and if necessary engage IRGC forces in the Gulf, taking into account that the IRGC is openly hostile towards the United States and that high-level Iranian officials have issued explicit threats against lawful US naval operations.

Collective Self-Defense   The United States is entitled under international law to join other states in collective self-defense. Iran's threat or use of force against Saudi Arabia, Bahrain, or Israel, for example, could lead any of them to ask the United States to join in their defense. The ICJ placed strict procedural limitations on this right in finding that the United States could not join in defending El Salvador against Nicaraguan-supported attacks. The United States has not accepted those limits, however, and in any case they may be inapplicable to the situations likely to arise as a result of IRGC aggression. The IRGC may, for example, assist Shia-led anti-government forces in Bahrain in a manner that would justify interception of shipments of arms. It has used force to gain control of the island of Abu Musa and other small but strategic islands near the Straits of Hormuz, despite claims to sovereignty by the United Arab Emirates; the United States could assist the UAE in having its claims to those islands resolved according to law rather than by the threat or use of force. If Israel requested US assistance in defending against Iranian support for attacks by Hezbollah, Hamas, or the IRGC itself, the United States could agree to join Israel in defending against such attacks.

Determining the precise parameters of US legal authority to join in the collective self-defense of states threatened or attacked by Iran cannot be done in advance. The United States and its allies could usefully warn Iran of the possible use of this authority, however. Iran would certainly worry about any possible exercise of US power on behalf of allies that Iran has bullied or treated as enemies.

Legitimacy of Defensive Measures Against the IRGC

Judging the legitimacy of using force requires an examination of factors beyond those considered in evaluating its legality. An action's legitimacy ultimately depends on how it is perceived by the relevant international community, not merely in terms of legal sufficiency. Although aspects of legality are related to legitimacy, especially necessity ("last resort") and proportionality, legitimacy requires consideration of additional factors widely recognized as relevant, including: seriousness of the threat; proper purpose; international support; confidence in the factual findings and conclusions upon which an action is based; and the balance of consequences, as in doing less harm than good.[16]

Applying these criteria to possible preventive military action against Iran's nuclear program, before it has developed a nuclear weapon, indicates that such an action would be viewed by most states as unprovoked and illegitimate. The threat posed by a nuclear-armed Iran would be extremely serious, and preventing nuclear proliferation is undoubtedly a proper purpose, as is the enforcement of UNSC resolutions ordering Iran to stop its nuclear-related activities. But Iran does not yet have nuclear weapons and may ultimately decide against developing them. Moreover, most states would probably agree that Iran has the "right" to have a peaceful nuclear-energy program, including enrichment.[17] Stronger economic sanctions, together with limited force, might convince Iran to negotiate an acceptable compromise.

In any event, it is impossible to know in advance whether a particular assault on Iran's nuclear program could satisfy the criterion of proportionality; extremely damaging consequences to non-combatants and the environment could result from the types of attacks that may be required. Few states would accept that preventive attacks for the purpose of destroying Iran's nuclear program could ever satisfy the most basic requirement of legitimacy—to do less harm than good; and many, if not most, experts believe that such attacks would ultimately be futile. Commentators have already begun to cite the "hypocrisy" of the US and other NPT nuclear powers for failing to live up to their obligation to eliminate all nuclear weapons.[18]

On the other hand, applying the same legitimacy-related criteria to defensive military actions against the IRGC indicates that such actions would readily meet the test of legitimacy. While the forms of aggression the IRGC has engaged in are potentially less devastating than the nuclear threat, they represent clearly illegal types of conduct that have inflicted substantial harm. The most significant difference between defensive actions against IRGC aggression and attacks on Iran's nuclear program is that the former have already happened and are continuing, while the latter has not yet reached a critical stage. The proportionality of defensive measures against particular IRGC targets can accurately be estimated, and targets that would pose disproportionate dangers of harm to non-combatants or the environment can be avoided. Attacks aimed at deterring IRGC aggression could be limited, for example, to targets that are less protected than nuclear sites, such as: arms shipments within Iran destined for Iranian surrogates; facilities associated with the IRGC and its Quds Force (including that Force's several isolated bases in the Persian Gulf); IRGC-controlled vessels and ports, trucks, cargo planes, and other facilities used to ship arms to surrogates and for terrorist actions; factories and storage facilities used to produce arms supplied to surrogates, including rockets and IEDs; IRGC units taking part in illegal activities, including training; and facilities used for any such activity. The IRGC bases at Abu Musa and Farsi Island (near Kuwait), Daniel Crist notes, "have long been key cogs in the Iranian military machine in the Persian Gulf."[19]

The task of overcoming Iran's defenses will be substantial, even for limited attacks on selected, relatively vulnerable targets; but US military analysts are confident that Iran's defensive capacities can be overcome without significant losses.[20] US military capacities have been stretched in Iraq and Afghanistan, and the United States is in a period of slow economic growth and high deficits. But defensive measures aimed at the IRGC would not even resemble the conflicts in Iraq and Afghanistan in terms of cost, and would largely, if not exclusively, be conducted from the air or sea; if successful at preventing Iranian weapons from reaching insurgents and terrorists, such measures could in fact accelerate the withdrawal of US forces from Afghanistan and increase the prospect of positive outcomes there and in Iraq.[21]

Covert Attacks

In Iran itself, recent attacks have taken place for which no state or group has taken responsibility and that appear to have been aimed by Israel and/or the US at Iran's nuclear program. Several persons described as nuclear scientists have been killed. Explosions have taken place at an Iranian missile center and at or near nuclear facilities. A computer worm called Stuxnet infiltrated computers used in the facilities, causing significant physical damage to enrichment equipment and setting back Iran's nuclear progress. A second computer attack, called "Flame," was launched for the same purpose.[22]

While an unlawful attack remains unlawful whether overt or covert, it does not follow that an attack that would be lawful if avowed becomes unlawful if conducted covertly. Covert attacks may serve the interests of international peace and security in some situations. By acting covertly, a state may, for example, be able to avoid escalating the hostility that exists between it and the state it attacks, thereby achieving some proper result without causing an armed conflict. Covert actions are routinely undertaken during armed conflict without any requirement that they be reported to the Security Council or otherwise.

On the other hand, covert actions have distinct disadvantages relative to overt ones explicitly undertaken in self-defense. A state's decision to refuse to acknowledge its responsibility for a use of force may indicate that it lacks confidence in the propriety of its conduct. Covert actions are more likely than overt ones to be undertaken without the internal scrutiny applied to actions that a state intends to avow. Nations that act covertly generally seek to avoid the UN Charter's requirement that actions in self-defense be reported to the Security Council, whereas a nation that acts overtly in self-defense is by definition willing to subject its decision to international scrutiny. And an overt action in self-defense at least makes clear the type of conduct the state exercising self-defense is seeking to deter.

The utility of covert measures thus far undertaken against Iran also remains uncertain. Covert attacks appear to have succeeded in setting back Iran's nuclear activities, but have failed to cause Iran to change course. They have led its leaders to resort to its own assassinations and cyber attacks,[23] and may make Iran even more determined to pursue its nuclear-related objectives. If the United States and/or Israel have been responsible for covert assassinations or cyber attacks on Iran's nuclear program, they should hardly be surprised when Iran resorts to similar activity.[24] Actions in self-defense for which the US assumes full responsibility, and which it justifies publicly and in the UN, would likely prove more effective in deterring IRGC aggression.

Balance of Consequences

The ultimate test of legitimacy—and of sensible security strategy—is whether the balance of consequences indicates that defensive actions aimed at deterring illegal IRGC conduct are likely to do less harm than good; whether, in short, they would achieve deterrence and enhance the prospects of peace, rather than result, for example, in a significant escalation of IRGC aggression or in a definitive decision by Iranian leadership to develop nuclear weapons.

While the pros and cons of attacking Iran's nuclear program have been widely examined and debated, the feasibility and consequences of taking limited, defensive actions against the IRGC have been ignored. Although every major foreign policy report on the Iranian threat supports the need to increase *pressure* on Iran, none explicitly considers limited uses of defensive force as a necessary and potentially useful means of creating such pressure.[25] Leaders and analysts who favor preventively attacking Iran's nuclear program have often noted that the United States has failed to respond against IRGC aggression.[26] But even in making that valid point, they have focused on the need to prevent Iran from acquiring nuclear weapons, and appear to regard the objective of deterring the IRGC as strategically inconsequential. Some may assume that any use of force against Iran is likely to be counterproductive by giving its leaders reason to acquire nuclear weapons rather than to curb IRGC conduct.

The option of using limited force in response to IRGC-sponsored attacks deserves to be considered and promptly embraced.[27] Using defensive force against the IRGC would provide the United States with useful strategic flexibility. It is sound strategy to exploit the full range of options available to curb the IRGC by means short of preventive attacks on nuclear sites. The difficulty of establishing the propriety, feasibility, and effectiveness of preventive military attacks on those sites makes attacking them unlikely at this time, and may ultimately lead the United States, and possibly Israel, to adopt a policy of containment, despite its risks. The legality, legitimacy, and feasibility of a policy of using defensive force against IRGC aggression, on the other hand, can be readily established. Actions in self-defense would have the limited objective of deterring aggression, and would require no exit strategy similar to what would be required for preventive attacks seeking to end Iran's nuclear program. Regardless of Iran's nuclear status, the United States must be defended, in order to preserve US credibility and deter IRGC aggression effectively. Defensive actions would also encourage Iran to negotiate in earnest, and could be undertaken without precluding the option of preventively attacking its nuclear facilities.

Using force to defend against IRGC attacks could cause the organization to escalate its support for insurgent and terrorist groups, attack the US with its own regular, military forces, or to speed up—rather than abandon—its development of nuclear weapons.[28] The IRGC's involvement in the attack on the Jewish Community Center in Argentina in 1994, for example, appears to have been in response to Israel's attacks on a Hezbollah leader in Lebanon, and recent attacks aimed at Israeli diplomats in Delhi and Thailand seem to have been launched in response to those on Iranian nuclear physicists.

Iran's missiles can reach Israel and Eastern Europe, and its naval assets (including Swedish speedboats, Russian submarines, North Korean torpedo and missile boats, and Chinese coastal and ship-borne cruise missiles) enable it to inflict considerable damage on US naval vessels and temporarily shut down the Persian Gulf, preventing the flow of oil from the area.[29] Iran's Admiral Habibollah Sayari boasted that "shutting the strait . . . is really easy, or as we say in Iran, easier than drinking a glass of water."[30]

It is doubtful, however, that the IRGC will escalate its illegal activities in response to limited US attacks undertaken in self-defense. Iranian leaders have staked a great deal on the nation's nuclear program, and might feel compelled to respond aggressively to an attack on that program—with all the collateral consequences. Iran obtains limited advantages, however, from its support through the IRGC for surrogate and terrorist attacks compared to the potential costs of escalation. The Iranian government wants to extend its influence in the Muslim world, and does so in part by damaging and embarrassing the United States. But Iran's influence in Iraq and Afghanistan, for example, depends less on the surrogate attacks it has abetted than on its allies in both places.

Iran may well have gained some advantages from IRGC support for attacks on US forces in Iraq and Afghanistan in that it is seen as having helped push the United States out of both countries by successfully supporting the killing of Americans. Helping to attack its enemies with impunity probably does enhance the IRGC's capacity to intimidate and gains it prestige within Iran. But the cost of pursuing such policies would be increased significantly if the United States were to hold the IRGC accountable for them. Iran has a substantial interest in avoiding direct confrontations that could prove embarrassing, create greater internal economic hardship, or increase domestic criticism and dissent. Unlike the widespread hostility within Iran that an attack on its nuclear-related facilities would presumably create, limited strikes on selected IRGC targets are likely to be viewed by many Iranians as the result of that group's foolishly aggressive policies; a wide swath of the public sees the IRGC and its Basij Force as corrupt and extremist.[31]

Iran is also unlikely to use its conventional military forces against the United States. Conventional confrontations would be costly for Iran, and it lacks the logistical and military capacity to project conventional power far beyond its borders. When Saddam Hussein attacked Iran, it defended itself valiantly; but it failed when it attempted to conquer Shiite areas in Southern Iraq. It has since then avoided conventional conflict, relying instead on IRGC support for surrogates and undercover operations, sometimes through its embassies. The one set of armed encounters Iran has had with the US Navy, in the Gulf in 1987 and, 1988,[32] caused it to cease mining the Gulf and attacking US-flagged vessels.[33]

Even assuming Iran would retaliate for US defensive actions against the IRGC by escalating support for surrogate and terrorist attacks, or by using its own military, the United States should nonetheless end its indulgence of IRGC aggression. The United States is ultimately at greater risk by allowing the IRGC to continue its current conduct than by defending against IRGC aggression. The record of US policy in dealing with al-Qaeda's attacks prior to 9/11 indicates how dangerous it can be to fail to respond against the sponsor of surrogate or terrorist attacks. Threats and indictments issued against al-Qaeda's leadership caused Osama bin Laden to conclude (and proclaim) that the United States was degenerate and weak,[34] and to conduct major attacks against American interests, including bombings of the World Trade Center (1993), of two US embassies in Africa (1998), of the USS *Cole* in Yemen (2000),[35] and ultimately of the World Trade Center and Pentagon (2001). Intelligence lapses may explain why US law enforcement agencies were unable to prevent the 9/11 attackers from achieving their objectives. But it was the US failure to respond in self-defense on al-Qaeda's known bases in Afghanistan, not any lapse of intelligence or information sharing, that allowed al-Qaeda to send its terrorists on their missions. The US failure to respond prior to the 9/11 attacks also enabled al-Qaeda, at its Afghanistan headquarters, to train more than 100,000 terrorists, who have been directly or indirectly involved in several major attacks in the US and other countries.

Allowing the IRGC to sponsor and conduct attacks on the United States with impunity seems in fact more likely to cause the IRGC to escalate its activities against and within the United States than a policy focused on response. US national security agencies have reported that the IRGC has recently been more willing to consider attacks on US territory, and is likely to implement them if the United States does not respond in a manner that makes them costly. National Intelligence Director James Clapper testified in January 2012 that the planned assassination of the Saudi ambassador in Washington indicates that Iran's leaders "have changed their calculus and are now more willing to conduct an attack in the United States in response to real or perceived actions that threaten the regime." The extent to which Iran is willing to sponsor attacks against the United States at home or abroad, he said, "probably will be shaped by Tehran's evaluation of the costs it bears for the plot against the ambassador as well as Iranian leaders' perceptions of the U.S. threats against the regime."[36]

The notion that IRGC-sponsored or -conducted attacks should be tolerated in order to avoid the threat of Iranian escalation is, in any event, fundamentally mistaken.[37] On that premise, the United States should not have killed Osama bin Laden, since (as Ayman al-Zawahiri has subsequently threatened) al-Qaeda is surely now attempting to make the US pay for that action. Al-Qaeda may in fact attempt to avenge bin Laden's death. But al-Qaeda has already been attempting to attack the US. Allowing Osama bin Laden to evade responsibility for his series of attacks could hardly be expected to have led him or al-Qaeda to *stop* attacking the United States. The US failure to act in self-defense against al-Qaeda after each of the attacks leading up to 9/11 indicates that, if anything, the opposite is true.

How Iran responds to legitimate exercises of self-defense would, in addition, provide important evidence as to the rationality of Iranian national-security decision-making. If Iran escalates its illegal activities in response to IRGC-provoked, legitimate acts of self-defense, the United States and the international community may be justified in concluding, as Dore Gold has suggested, that the Islamic regime "could very well be immune to deterrence and the threat of full scale retaliation should it employ nuclear weapons."[38] Limited strikes aimed at IRGC resources and operations could also encourage criticism and resistance against IRGC policies from less radical elements of the Iranian national security community and society. In addition, once the United States makes clear its intent to use force against Iran in self-defense, China, Russia, and other states may be more receptive to approving stronger economic sanctions against Iran in order to demonstrate that the use of force is unnecessary.[39]

Current US policy may in fact be based on the notion that attacking Iran, even in self-defense, would serve to convince Iranian leaders that they do indeed need nuclear weapons. The US decision to criminally charge the individuals responsible for the IRGC plot to kill the Saudi ambassador may well indicate (and will in any event be seen by Iran as reflecting) a willingness to absorb Iranian attacks without responding with force, thereby convincing Iran that it is safe from reprisal even without nuclear weapons. Secretary of State Hillary Clinton, for example, has emphatically denied any US involvement in the covert attacks within Iran aimed at nuclear scientists, stating on January 11, 2012: "I want to categorically deny any United States involvement in any kind of act of violence inside Iran."[40] However it was intended, this sweeping statement may have reassured Iran that the United States has no intention of attacking any target on its territory, for any reason.[41]

A policy of not attacking Iran in order to avoid causing it to decide to develop nuclear weapons would be based on the premise that Iran wants nuclear weapons only to ensure its security from attack. That premise is naïve at best. Iran is seeking nuclear weapons to increase its influence and impunity in implementing its radical and far-reaching political agenda.[42] It makes no sense, moreover, to treat

Iran as if it already has a nuclear weapon in the hope that it will conclude that it does not need one. Nor is it safe to assume that allowing the IRGC to support and engage in conventional and terrorist attacks with impunity will be more likely to cause Iran's leaders to give up their nuclear program; rather, such indulgence is more likely to lead them to acquire nuclear weapons on the assumption that they will not be prevented from doing so.[43] A demonstration that the United States is prepared to use force in self-defense against IRGC aggression would tend to undermine any such assumption, and that policy could cause Iran to conclude that its effort to acquire nuclear weapons might be prevented or might not be worth the increased cost likely to result.

General Martin Dempsey, chairman of the Joint Chiefs of Staff, said in an interview on December 20, 2011, that his "biggest worry is that they [Iran] will miscalculate our resolve," which will mean "we are drawn into conflict."[44] General Dempsey's perceptive comment reflects a classic concern in strategic calculations. But it is a concern that can be brought on by misleading an enemy as to one's willingness to defend itself by acting with excessive caution or weakness. The US failure to respond effectively to Iranian nonnuclear misconduct is precisely the type of conduct likely to cause Iran to make that miscalculation. Iran could reasonably assume that, if the United States is unprepared to use limited force against manageable targets associated with *actual* but limited-scale aggression, it is unlikely to use the far greater amount of force required to destroy the many difficult targets associated with a nuclear program that is still only a *potential* threat.

The Iran Project Report identifies several factors that could well constitute "costs" of a policy of attacking Iran for the purpose of preventing it from developing nuclear weapons. Those factors are largely inapplicable to limited actions against selected IRGC targets for the purpose of self-defense. Actions in self-defense would be more feasible than preventive attacks, as explained above, and far less likely to be opposed by allies and the Muslim world. By definition, moreover, the right to defend the United States against Iranian aggression must when necessary be exercised in support of US security, regardless of its popularity within the international community or of the reaction such steps may provoke from Iran itself.

Perhaps most significantly, defending against IRGC aggression may well provide the United States with the additional dimension of pressure on Iran necessary to achieve diplomatic progress. To push back against IRGC aggression is more likely to lead Iran to negotiate in good faith and with greater flexibility. Taking on the IRGC for sponsoring attacks on the United States may also enable the American government to adopt the principles used in negotiating with the Soviet Union, discussed in the next chapter, that would permit sustained, potentially beneficial engagement with Iran and help defuse the current crisis.

CHAPTER 5

Beyond Strength: Effective Diplomacy

President Reagan and Secretary Shultz were determined to exploit the opportunities for engagement with the Soviet Union that became available due in part to the administration's firm reactions to Soviet misconduct. To do so, the Reagan Administration deliberately adopted and applied a set of negotiating principles that proved effective. These principles—rhetorical restraint, regime engagement, limited linkage, a broad agenda, and forum flexibility—helped to secure advantageous agreements in several areas and ultimately created the environment in which the Soviet regime did in fact change.

By contrast, and in part because of the weakness and inconsistency of US policy towards Iran, neither the Reagan Administration nor any subsequent US government has applied these principles in conducting US/Iranian negotiations. As a result, America's US/Iranian diplomacy has been markedly unsuccessful.

Rhetorical Restraint

The Reagan/Shultz strategy for diplomacy with the Soviet Union included two forms of rhetorical restraint: a decision not to "crow," i.e., not to boast or take credit, when the Soviets agreed to do something the United States had sought; and a policy of avoiding general threats, for example, that Soviet behavior was "unacceptable" when no concrete plan of action existed to prevent or counter the "unacceptable" conduct.

The anti-crowing policy was implemented in 1983 after a private meeting with Ambassador Anatoly Dobrynin, at which President Reagan urged the Soviet Union to be more responsive on human rights issues. He asked Dobrynin to help resolve the problem created when several Pentecostals took refuge in the US embassy in Moscow, promising Dobrynin that, if something positive were done for the group, the United States would not boast about it.[1] Dobrynin considered the promise significant, as he later cautioned Shultz that the "special subject" of the Pentecostals should be handled "privately," so the Soviet government could allow them to leave the country without incurring internal criticism.

Some members of the Reagan Administration wanted to embarrass the Soviet leadership, and sought every possible occasion to trumpet US successes. But Reagan concluded that it was more important to resolve a concrete issue of humanitarian concern than to take advantage of a Soviet accommodation. When the Pentecostals were allowed to leave Russia, the United States expressed its "appreciation" for the Soviet action and took no credit for their departure.[2]

President Reagan reiterated this policy at the negotiation in Reykjavik, Iceland, in 1986, when he assured Secretary Mikhael Gorbachev that the US would not advance human rights issues as "demands" and "would never take credit for" progress on such issues:

> The President . . . had no intention of saying publicly that he had demanded anything from Gorbachev in terms of such issues as family reunification and religious persecution. But he did want to urge Gorbachev to move forward in this area, since it was a major factor domestically in limiting how far the President could go in cooperation with the Soviet Union. . . . We would continue to provide lists of

people we had reason to believe wanted to depart. And if the Soviets loosened up, we would not exploit it. We would simply express our appreciation.[3]

The United States also allowed the Soviets to avoid appearing to have capitulated to US demands in handling the exchange of the Soviet spy, Gennadi Zacharov (who was set up by the FBI), for the US reporter, Nicholas Daniloff (who was set up by the KGB). The Soviets wanted to trade their spy for the US reporter, though they knew that Daniloff had been drawn into a compromising position by the negligence of US intelligence officials. Secretary Shultz accepted the trade the Soviets wanted, but secured an informal commitment from Foreign Minister Eduard Shevardnadze to release some important dissidents at a later point.[4] The US allowed the Soviets to take separate credit for releasing the additional dissidents, once again preferring to achieve a valuable result and to build trust rather than take public credit for the fact that the Zacharov/Daniloff exchange was in reality more favorable to the US than it appeared.

The United States has had little to crow about when it comes to convincing Iran to alter Iranian conduct. Nonetheless, it has taken public credit whenever possible. When Iran released the US diplomats it had held hostage for 444 days immediately after President Reagan was sworn into office, Administration spokesmen did nothing to negate the impression that Iran had acted out of fear of Ronald Reagan. Iran's leaders were eager to rebut any such inference. They had already agreed, in the Algiers Accords, to free the hostages in exchange for the release of billions of dollars of Iranian assets, but had delayed the release to spite outgoing President Carter (whom they "despised").[5]

The danger of taking public credit for Iranian concessions can be seen in the reaction of US officials to Iran's agreement in principle, in October 2009, to transfer a significant portion of its low-enriched uranium to Russia and France in exchange for uranium enriched to about 20 percent for medical purposes.[6] This agreement would have converted about 70 percent of the LEU then under Iranian control to solid fuel rods that are extremely difficult to turn into weapons-grade material, and it would have also kept Iran from gaining the experience of enriching to the 20 percent level. *Time* magazine reported that "Administration and European officials presented Iran's moves as a response to mounting pressure from the West. . . ."[7] President Obama warned, moreover, that the United States would stop talking to Iran and seek more sanctions if Iran did not implement the accord and also allow inspection of a newly revealed plant in Qom.[8]

Iranian officials who approved the fuel-swap agreement immediately faced domestic attacks for making that concession. They correctly argued that the agreement advanced Iran's interests; for one thing, it implicitly accepted the legitimacy of Iran's enrichment activities. But they could not reverse the impression created by US statements that Iran had made major concessions and would face sanctions if it failed to follow through. President Ahmadinejad, who was in the midst of an election campaign, was denounced for submitting to US pressure. His "liberal" opponent, Mir Hossein Mousavi, described the fuel-swap agreement as "astonishing" and "the result of adventurism and bypassing national principles and national interests in foreign policy." If the Geneva deal were implemented, Mousavi said, "it will mean the efforts of countless Iranian scientists will go to waste; and if not implemented, it will prepare the social grounds for imposing more sanctions on the country." The Iranian press reported: "Mousavi described the policy as kowtowing to the United States."[9] Ahmadinejad pointed out that his policies had taken Iran much further in mastering the enrichment process than any past government. But he soon backed away from the deal, offering unacceptable alternatives.[10]

Further economic sanctions were imposed, but they did not prevent Iran from proceeding unilaterally to enrich to 20 percent, thereby virtually ensuring its ability to enrich to the level needed for a weapon. While Iran has often backed away from concessions, as part of its strategy of delay, US crowing over its initial agreement may have played a part in making the nuclear-swap deal domestically unpalatable.

The Reagan Administration also attempted to avoid empty rhetoric in its Soviet dealings. The president robustly criticized the Soviet system and its frequently reprehensible conduct (such as the shooting down of the KAL airliner), and called for more responsible and humane Soviet policies. But his Administration avoided threats that could raise unrealistic expectations and diminish US credibility.

Empty threats and claims have been common, however, in US dealings with Iran. Every administration since the Islamic Republic was formed has expressly or implicitly threatened the use of force if Iran continued to support terrorism or develop the capacities to make a nuclear bomb; every such threat has failed to alter Iran's or its IRGC's conduct, yet this repeated defiance has gone unchecked and unchallenged—at least in an effective way. Similar threats were ineffective in keeping North Korea from developing a nuclear weapon and engaging in other dangerous misconduct, including attacks on South Korea. Every administration has also warned that crippling economic sanctions would be imposed on Iran, despite knowing that the adoption of tough, multilateral sanctions was unlikely given the opposition of key nations on and outside the Security Council.

Regime Engagement

In diplomacy, the Reagan Administration engaged the Soviet regime as a sovereign entity entitled to its rights under the UN Charter, and refrained from overt or covert activities to bring about regime change through force or other improper means. Despite the Soviet Union's stature and power, Soviet leaders and diplomats repeatedly insisted that their nation's dealings with the United States be conducted on the basis of "equality and equal security";[11] and while they objected to US criticism of the Soviet system, they acknowledged the difference between open, verbal advocacy of democratic values and human rights, and covert support for violence or regime change.

Regime engagement did not prevent President Reagan from expressing his disapproval of the Soviet regime and predicting its demise. He condemned the Soviet Union as an "Evil Empire," and predicted that the Communist system was destined for the garbage heap of history.[12] Secretary Gorbachev, although unhappy with Reagan's blunt criticisms, did not treat them as inconsistent with peaceful coexistence. He said at Reykjavik, for example: "The President's remarks showed that they differed fundamentally in their basic conceptions of the world. But the two leaders seemed to agree that each side had the right to organize its society according to its own philosophical or religious beliefs."[13]

Many in Congress, and in the Reagan Administration itself, opposed treating the Soviet regime as legitimate even for the purpose of diplomatic engagement. They believed that the United States should refuse to extend any form of respect to the regime in order to speed its demise. Secretary Shultz and the president shared the hope of a Soviet demise, the quicker the better. But Shultz was convinced—and convinced the president and Congress—to oppose Soviet misconduct by responding directly, through military and political pressure, rather than by refusing to engage the regime diplomatically. He believed then as now "that strength and diplomacy are not alternatives; rather they complement each other."[14] Instead of treating the Soviet regime as illegitimate or seeking regime change through covert operations, the Reagan Administration settled on a two-track policy of simultaneously confronting Soviet aggression with American strength, while seeking diplomatic engagement with a sovereign that was entitled to the rights and respect associated with standard international diplomatic practice.

US policy toward the Iranian regime has been very different from the Reagan/Shultz approach to the Soviet Union. Rather than confronting Iran's frequent, egregious misconduct directly through assertive actions of self-defense and other forms of military pressure, the United States has repeatedly refused to engage diplomatically with Iran, largely restricting its response to the imposition of (ineffective) economic sanctions. Members of Congress, several administrations, and many experts have advocated or predicted "regime change" in Iran as the only effective way to alter its conduct and policies, with Congress at one point authorizing $18 million for covert operations designed to promote the alteration.[15] This legislation was as ineffective as all the other wishful thinking; it led Iran to authorize some $20 million to combat such efforts, followed soon thereafter by the Khobar Towers bombing.

An example of how regime engagement was applied in dealing with the Soviets as compared to Iran is the different way in which the United States has treated the Soviet Union and Iran with respect to sovereign immunities. The United States enforced, over Soviet objections, the narrowed view of sovereign immunity adopted in the Foreign Sovereign Immunity Act (FSIA).[16] The Soviets initially refused to appear in the US courts when sued, allowing default judgments to be entered in several pending cases, including one for $100 million for failing to pay amounts due under Czarist bonds issued prior to the Soviet Revolution.[17] These developments disrupted US/Soviet relations at a time when important diplomatic initiatives were underway.

As Legal Adviser, I convinced the Soviets to appear in the relevant US courts and to assert sovereign immunity in the manner provided for in the FSIA, agreeing that the United States would also appear to state its position on the immunity questions at issue. The Soviets were able in this manner to protect their sovereign rights as defined by the FSIA.[18] Some plaintiffs and lawyers in those and similar cases were unhappy that the United States had "helped" the Soviet Union secure dismissals of legal actions. But dismissals occurred only where legally appropriate; legally sufficient claims were allowed to proceed. Secretary Shultz deliberately used this issue (and others) to demonstrate US acceptance of the Soviet regime's legal rights, and our cooperation enhanced the trust being simultaneously established in other ongoing US/Soviet negotiations. At no point did the United States ever advocate that the Soviet Union should be deprived of immunity because it had supported terrorism or had violated some established principle of human rights or international law.[19]

The US has taken a different approach in handling disputes concerning Iran's sovereign rights. Congress amended the FSIA in 1996 to allow suits by victims against state sponsors of terrorist acts, defined to include violations of treaties covering torture, extrajudicial killing, aircraft sabotage, hostage taking, and other crimes. President Clinton signed the legislation, prompting the filing of hundreds of suits, primarily against Iranian and Cuban officials and agencies.[20] Iran has in general refused to appear in these suits, leading to default judgments amounting to many billions of dollars; judgments issued for Iran's responsibility for the 1983 Marine barracks bombing alone amount to $8.8 billion.[21]

These judgments have been impossible to enforce against Iranian assets still within the United States, such as diplomatic facilities, which are immune from such actions, and plaintiffs are competing with each other to seize funds to cover small portions of the judgments they have secured from debts to Iran by US banks and businesses.[22] Congress has provided funds to pay certain judgments against Iran from the US Treasury, which it has done for judgments against Cuba, on the dubious theory that sums the American people pay to plaintiffs and their lawyers will someday be collected from Iran or from the proceeds of sales of its assets.[23] Lawyers have pressed for the sale of any and all Iranian assets to satisfy the judgments they have obtained, with Congress' support, but the executive branch has pushed back in order to preserve immunity for US diplomatic accounts and facilities. Plaintiffs' attorneys are also seeking to overcome another, traditional obstacle to collecting on these judgments: the need to prove, when assets are seized, that the assets are in fact the property of the government agency responsible.[24]

Punishing Iran, particularly the IRGC, for committing or supporting terrorist attacks that kill or injure Americans would be a welcome development. That is what this book recommends. The United States should defend its citizens against such attacks, not only for the sake of those citizens, but also because that policy would project the strength needed for deterrence and effective negotiations. Refusing to accept Iran's sovereign immunities, however, is a costly and feeble substitute for the exercise of self-defense. The United States has a strong and abiding interest in relying on the doctrine of sovereign immunity to protect its own government, officials, former officials, and diplomatic properties from suits in foreign courts. Narrowing Iran's immunities (or those of its responsible officials) makes sense in areas where an international consensus exists that states and officials have no immunity from judicial accountability, as under the Genocide Convention. But unprecedented steps to remove Iranian immunities, and efforts to reach the diplomatic assets of Iran within US control, are inconsistent with the US interest in preserving such immunities, and indicate to Iran that the US remains unwilling to engage the Islamic regime on the basis of sovereign equality.

Demonstrating strength by refusing to accept the Islamic regime for purposes of effective diplomatic engagement is a misplaced notion. The policies of denying Iran its diplomatic and sovereign rights, and of advocating regime change through improper means, actually reflect weakness in the US posture.[25] These policies are the product of frustration in Congress and elsewhere that stems from the failure of US administrations to counter IRGC support for surrogate attacks and terrorism with appropriate measures of response. Posturing about "regime change," or diluting traditional practices of international diplomacy, are not meaningful substitutes for action. As Henry Kissinger noted in 2006:

Focusing on regime change as the road to denuclearization confuses the issue. The United States should oppose nuclear weapons in North

Korea and Iran regardless of the government that builds them. The diplomacy appropriate to denuclearization is comparable to the containment policy that helped win the Cold War: no preemptive challenge to the external security of the adversary, but firm resistance to attempts to project its power abroad and reliance on domestic forces to bring about internal change. It was precisely such a nuanced policy that caused President Ronald Reagan to invite Soviet leader Leonid Brezhnev to a dialogue within weeks of labeling the Soviet Union as the evil empire.[26]

Limited Linkage

President Reagan decided to negotiate with the Soviet Union despite its illegal and inhumane activities. This decision was controversial. Many officials in his Administration, as well as members of Congress, opposed negotiating with the Soviet Union because of its serious misconduct in one area or another. But President Reagan's decision was an essential prerequisite to successful engagement—not because supporters of linking negotiations to conduct were exaggerating the Soviets' misbehavior, but because their misbehavior was so consistently reprehensible that a strong linkage policy would have made negotiations impossible.

In briefing Congress in 1983 on the Administration's plan to limit linkage, Secretary Shultz candidly agreed with Soviet skeptics that increased diplomatic engagement would not improve Soviet behavior, even if progress were made in the overall relationship or on specific issues. But improper Soviet acts in each area of activity, he contended, must be met with US opposition and pressure *in those areas*, not by refusing to engage on all issues, including those on which the United States itself wished to engage. "Linkage," he explained, "was inhibiting our disposition to move forcefully and, ironically, often seemed to be turned on its head by the Soviets . . . to threaten that the relationship would suffer if we undertook some action that they opposed."[27] Congress allowed the Administration to implement this strategy, no doubt because the president had gained credibility through his determined resistance to Soviet aggression. The United States was thus able to maintain negotiations with the Soviet Union that served US interests, regardless of persistent Soviet misconduct.

No such arrangement has even been attempted regarding US/Iranian negotiations, probably because no administration has demonstrated credibility in resisting Iranian aggression. Instead, every US administration has at some point resorted to refusing to negotiate with Iran because of its egregiously improper conduct. Linking those two has become a substitute for confronting the misconduct itself. Just as Secretary Shultz predicted with regard to US/Soviet dealings, this policy of linkage has made consistent engagement with Iran impossible, since Iranian leaders have refused to stop enrichment, and continue to support terrorism and to oppose efforts to make peace between the Palestinians and Israel. As a result, the United States has deprived itself of the opportunity to engage Iran when it is in the US interest to do so, while having no discernible impact on the Iranian misconduct that linkage is intended to curb.

The single instance in which the United States defended itself against IRGC aggression instead of invoking linkage as a substitute—in the Gulf in 1987 and 1988—convinced Iran to stop its then-active practice of attacking US-flagged vessels and mining the Gulf. That result certainly supports the view that armed resistance can successfully deter IRGC aggression without causing Iran to terminate a useful negotiation.[28]

During that time, I was negotiating with the Iranians in The Hague and was ordered by Michael Armacost, Undersecretary for Political and Military Affairs, to cancel a scheduled meeting. My Iranian counterpart, Dr. Eftekhar, asked why the US had cancelled. I replied because Iran had put mines into the Gulf. He predictably denied that Iran had mined the Gulf, but argued that the mining dispute was separate from our negotiation, and said in effect that he and I were the only bridge between our countries, why burn it down? I reported this exchange to Undersecretary Armacost. Impressed by the equanimity with which Iran responded to the US attacks on its ships and platforms, he let me go back to The Hague, where Dr. Eftekhar and I continued to make progress in legal and other discussions.

Undersecretary Armacost felt no need to link our negotiation to Iran's conduct, since President Reagan had responded in kind to Iran's use of force in the Gulf. And that action did not cause Iran to terminate discussions in The Hague; in fact, Iran's negotiator urged that they be continued.

The Reagan Administration abandoned linkage in the Iran/Contra Affair, negotiating arms sales to Iran and offering a new relationship in exchange for the release of US hostages seized in Lebanon. But this policy was in effect an attempt to bribe Iran, not to confront IRGC misconduct. The plan to sell Iran arms in exchange for the release of hostages stemmed from weakness, not resolve, and Iran understood that. The effort achieved nothing and greatly damaged US credibility.

Linkage was invoked to reject engagement during the George H.W. Bush administration—in December 1991, after President Rafsanjani assisted in securing release of all the remaining hostages seized in Lebanon.[29] The events leading up to the release are described above, but it is relevant here that Rafsanjani's decision to assist in securing the hostage release probably stemmed from several factors, including President Bush's announcement in his inaugural address that the United States would appreciate and long remember help rendered in securing the release of its hostages—that "good will begets good will."[30]

Clearly, the Iranian president's assistance was based on the expectation that the hostage release would lead to an improvement in US/Iranian relations. But linkage once again prevented the US from persisting in a policy of engagement that was having positive results. The IRGC predictably supplied ample grounds for complaint by continuing, both before and after the hostage release, to arm anti-Israel terrorist groups, assassinate enemies of the Islamic regime in foreign countries, ruthlessly suppress internal opposition, and commit heinous acts of terrorism—in particular, in 1992, to use Iran's Embassy in Buenos Aires to assist Hezbollah agents in bombing the Israeli Embassy.[31] These and other activities led the Bush Administration, despite the hostage releases, to decide against further engagement with Iran. The president did not violate any legal or even moral commitment in denying any benefit to Iran for securing the release of hostages whose seizure it had probably supported; and he cannot be faulted for taking into account the risk of rewarding Iran just prior to an impending US presidential election. But his decision was nonetheless disappointing to those who had worked to set the stage for a possibly constructive engagement between the two states.[32]

Although Iran remained eager to engage, all political discussions ceased, and even the claims negotiations at The Hague slowed almost to a halt, forcing Iran to spend more than the next two decades litigating, rather than having its claims settled for amounts that would have served the interests of both sides.

Iran should certainly have been punished for the IRGC's continued support for terrorism and other misconduct. But US refusal to negotiate with Iranian leaders could hardly be regarded as an effective remedy. As in other situations, linkage did nothing to make up for the failure of the United States (and the international community) to respond effectively to IRGC aggression. What linkage did do was cause the United States to miss an opportunity to pursue improved relations with an Iranian leader who acknowledged in public that Iran had helped release the US hostages in an effort to demonstrate good will and thereby improve US/Iranian relations, and who paid a major price domestically for misjudging US intentions.[33]

Another episode of refusing to respond to Iran's expressed willingness to engage broadly due to linkage took place after the United States had defeated the Taliban in Afghanistan and Saddam Hussein in Iraq. The initial overwhelming success of American forces in both places appears to have led Iran to cooperate in the process of securing agreement on the Karzai candidacy and other arrangements the United States supported. When Iranian negotiators sought to continue their contacts with US Ambassador Dobbins on a broader range of issues, Dobbins sought approval to respond positively. "It is time," he said, "to apply to Iran the policies which won the Cold War, liberated the Warsaw Pact, and reunited Europe: détente and containment, communication whenever possible, and confrontation whenever necessary."[34] The George W. Bush Administration, however, regarded the Islamic regime as unworthy of engagement given its continued support for terrorism.[35] Once again, linkage proved no substitute for strength; refusing to negotiate did nothing to deter IRGC support for attacks on US soldiers in Iraq and Afghanistan or its other illegal activities, and the opportunity to engage was lost.

A Broad Agenda

The US/Soviet negotiating agenda during the Reagan presidency included issues that both sides wanted to discuss. The parties divided them into four broad categories: arms control, human rights, regional matters, and bilateral relations. This comprehensive list enhanced the prospect of productive exchanges and progress on at least some issues at every meeting. While US/Soviet negotiations were intended above all to reduce the threat posed by nuclear weapons, the parties also pursued many less complicated matters on which they could more readily reach agreements. Among those matters were improved commercial relations, expanded cultural and educational exchanges, and progress on human rights.

For years, US/Iranian negotiations have been (with the exception of legal claims) almost exclusively aimed at convincing Iran to stop enriching uranium and comply with its nuclear-related obligations. Other issues have been discussed, especially by the European states leading the P5+1 negotiations, but only for the purpose of establishing in general terms the quid pro quo for Iran's agreement and compliance on the nuclear issues. As a practical matter, this has meant that Iran has been unable to obtain the actual implementation of agreements reached on any of its own objectives, because it has been unwilling to give up its position on the issue that matters most to the US, its nuclear program. Iran must have inferred from such a negotiating posture, as North Korea did, that its leverage with the United States is limited to the threat its nuclear program creates and that agreeing to settle the nuclear issue would leave Iran with little, if any, further leverage unless it repeatedly reneges and renegotiates, as North Korea has done.

A broader negotiating agenda with Iran, similar to that adopted by the United States and Soviet Union in their Reagan-era negotiations, would have greater potential for progress than the narrow approach followed thus far. Each party should be permitted to identify the areas of concern it wants addressed, and a procedure should be established that ensures that all significant issues are discussed. Iran would no doubt seek agreements on many issues unrelated to its nuclear agenda, including its substantial claims in The Hague Tribunal,[36] regional matters, territorial disputes, the suspension of sanctions, membership in the World Trade Organization, commercial purchases such as airplane parts, and educational and cultural exchanges. The US would insist, as with the Soviets, on discussing at every meeting the critical issues of Iran's nuclear activities, Iranian support of surrogate and terrorist attacks, Iran's hostility toward Israel and the Middle East peace process, and the suppression of human and political rights within Iran. Including human rights in US/Iran negotiations is not only appropriate in principle; it is also strongly supported by many Iranians as well as by influential nations and groups in the international community.[37]

The US should go beyond only *discussing* the issues Iran wishes addressed; it should also be prepared whenever possible to reach and immediately *implement* mutually beneficial agreements on those issues rather than having their implementation conditioned on a satisfactory agreement related to Iran's nuclear activities. That approach would provide benefits to Iran based on its willingness to alter its conduct in ways that serve US interests and international peace and security. It could also establish between the countries a relationship that has multiple dimensions and a record of concrete agreements, which in turn might facilitate an arrangement to bring Iran's nuclear activities under credible controls.[38]

Forum Flexibility

US flexibility as to the place, level, and format for negotiations with the Soviet Union was another aspect of the successful strategy used during the Reagan Administration.[39] Secretary Shultz exploited numerous channels through which trustworthy diplomats and private individuals worked with Soviet officials on both governmental and commercial matters. The two nations met at times at the highest level, with much fanfare and many pre-negotiated outcomes. But teams at lower levels did most of the work, usually in confidence.

By contrast, with the exception of the confidential discussions conducted in The Hague and on a few other occasions, negotiations between Iran and the United States have been staged for public effect, with opening ceremonies covered by reporters and with cameras recording the parties' predictably hostile statements—made to assure each side's domestic constituency that it had no intention of agreeing to accept what the other side was publicly promising to demand. In these statements US negotiators have routinely threatened that sanctions will be imposed if Iran fails to agree to stop enrichment. Iranian negotiators have invariably stated that under no circumstances would they agree to compromise their "right" to enrich uranium and to use nuclear materials for other peaceful purposes.

Iranian leaders see these publicly staged meetings not as genuine negotiations, but as vehicles used by the United States to establish

Iran's intransigence and thereby to build the political consensus within the Security Council for increasingly severe economic sanctions. To avoid sanctions, Iran has at times agreed temporarily to suspend enrichment, or to allow an inspection. But the concessions have all later been withdrawn, resulting in four rounds of Security Council sanctions that have had an increasing impact on Iran's economy but have nonetheless not altered Iranian conduct. At this stage, negotiations would seem more promising if they took place in a context that did not require the parties to make pre-negotiation claims or threats, or publicly to dismiss proposals that, although unacceptable as presented, might serve as a basis for progress in a confidential setting.[40]

While private interlocutors were used successfully in certain aspects of the US/Soviet dealings in the 1980s, efforts to rely on private individuals in US/Iranian negotiations have proved ineffective and sometimes embarrassing.[41] Individuals given such roles have failed to act responsibly. Both states have, on the other hand, successfully used as interlocutors the governments of Algeria, Germany, Japan, and Switzerland, all of whom have performed in a professional, reliable, and discreet manner. The United States and Iran could also pursue direct, private negotiations in The Hague, or through the sort of exchange the Iranians proposed to Ambassador Dobbins. The parties should be prepared to utilize any reliable method of negotiating that avoids public encounters likely to preclude constructive outcomes.

Conclusion

Whether or not the current strategy of coupling economic sanctions with multilateral negotiations convinces Iran to modify its nuclear program adequately to alleviate security concerns, the United States should adopt as an alternative to preventive attack or containment a strategy based on defending against the IRGC's support of surrogate and terrorist attacks on the United States, its interests, and its allies.

Defending against IRGC aggression is directly related to the ultimate objective of convincing Iran to accept necessary limits on its nuclear program. To begin with, why would Iran take seriously US threats regarding a nuclear program that has not yet led to the development of a nuclear weapon, when the US has taken no action to curb the IRGC from conducting its fully developed, thirty-year, ongoing, and damaging programs of arming surrogates to actually attack the United States and even engaging in terrorist actions within the US capital? Failing to act against IRGC aggression has led Iran to conclude that, as with North Korea, the option of using force to prevent the development of nuclear weapons will be left "on the table," where it has ritualistically been placed by every recent US president.

In addition to serving its essential deterrent purpose, defending against Iranian aggression would lead Iran to seek meaningful negotiations with the United States rather than to escalate illegal IRGC activities. Iran reacted to the American navy's Gulf operations in the late 1980s, and to the US interventions in Iraq and Afghanistan, by seeking broader diplomatic engagement with the United States.

The need for strength in conducting diplomacy with a belligerent, revolutionary power, like the Islamic Republic or the Soviet Union, stems from the nature of the result being sought. It is futile to seek agreement with such powers in the ordinary sense of the word, that is, with the two sides acting in good faith making compromises to resolve a disagreement. What negotiators must seek instead in such cases, as Henry Kissinger has explained, is the creation of an "'objective' situation [that] is ratified by the settlement."[1] The purpose of responding to the limited war the IRGC has waged against the United States and the West is to make clear that the war may no longer be pursued safely, and indeed that its pursuit would be costly beyond any value it could confer. Iran, like the Soviet Union, sees no value in granting concessions; agreements are made by such regimes only when circumstances demand.

Strength alone, while indispensable, will be insufficient to create a diplomatic process that succeeds in convincing Iran to abandon the use of force, terror, and ultimately the military dimension of its nuclear program. To succeed diplomatically, the United States will have to make substantial modifications to the practices it has applied in US/Iranian negotiations. In the present political and diplomatic environment, no administration could convince Congress to support negotiations with Iran on the basis of the principles applied by the Reagan Administration in dealing with the Soviet Union. But defending against IRGC aggression could provide the credibility needed to secure congressional support for negotiating with Iran under the same principles.

Would a two-track approach of strength and diplomacy be effective in dealing with Iran? One cannot know in advance. But, despite the significant differences between the Soviet and Islamic regimes, the principles on which sound defense and effective diplomacy are based should be equally applicable to Iran as it was to the Soviet Union. Both Russia and Iran have deep historical roots and diplomatic experience. Iran has been no more aggressive than the Soviets were in attempting to achieve its objectives and spread its ideology. Iranian leaders are no less likely to be affected by a strong response to their misconduct than the Soviets were, and also no less likely than the Soviets to react negatively to demands that threaten their international legitimacy and domestic standing.

The aversion of many US (and other) political leaders and national security experts to "negotiating" with Iran is based on the consistent failure of the United States to base its diplomacy on strength. The diplomacy that this book supports is the type Ambassador Chester A. Crocker practiced in leading the United States effort to end racism in South Africa, in which the negotiating process is treated as "the engine that converts raw energy and tangible power into meaningful political results."[2] That sort of diplomacy with Iran has worked on the few occasions it has been tried, and would have a far greater prospect of success than diplomacy that is divorced from the reality that Iran is killing Americans with impunity.

The Iranian style of negotiating differs from that of the Soviets; Americans are more accustomed to the dry sarcasm and directness of the Soviets than the exaggeration and sometimes feigned sincerity of the Iranians. Among negotiators, a larger cultural gap exists between Iranians (particularly those who claim to be guided by religious doctrine) and Americans than the one that prevailed in President Reagan's time between Soviets and Americans. But US officials come from diverse backgrounds, and there are diplomats on both sides who can overcome such differences.

US leaders would do well in any event to temper their reliance on Iran "experts" in making decisions that relate to the protection of essential national interests. Every president has one duty above all: to safeguard the American people. Failing to defend America against IRGC aggression based on speculation that a particular Iranian leader or group might be offended by such actions may not only be wrong, but may also end up being counterproductive. The failure to respond to IRGC aggression to avoid the danger of alienating President Khatami was a mistake. The lack of response enhanced IRGC power and influence, which the IRGC used to prevent Khatami from improving US/Iranian relations and ultimately to destroy any influence he was able to wield.

Equally mistaken is an approach that fails to defend against IRGC aggression on the theory that limited, defensive uses of force would be inconsequential in dealing with the nuclear threat. The legality, legitimacy, and effectiveness of a policy of limited, defensive uses of force give such a policy significant advantages relative to resorting to preventive attacks, which would inevitably be criticized as "unprovoked." And the failure to take defensive measures will continue to convey the impression, true or false, that the United States and the West will not go beyond economic sanctions in attempting to convince Iran to abandon its nuclear weapons program.

US analysts have observed that Iranians tend to seek concessions "up front," without giving assurances that they will provide any quid pro quo. Pocketing concessions is something negotiators from all cultures love to do. The technique can readily be countered by offering relatively modest concessions until Iran has reciprocated at an adequate level. Iranians are also inclined to stretch out negotiations, to engage in verbal dexterity that masks their intentions, to repeatedly revisit issues that appeared to be settled, and to treat negotiations like a Middle Eastern marketplace, all of which can be frustrating. But these qualities are characteristics of negotiators with various cultural backgrounds; they demand patience, firmness, and good humor on the part of the negotiators across the table. Iranian diplomats are as capable of calculating their national interests and reaching binding agreements as the diplomats of any state, as indicated by the many settlement agreements reached between the United States and Iran since the Algiers Accords. It is baseless to assume that Iranians, because of their culture or religious doctrines, are any less likely to abide by their agreements than other states; agreements by any state can ultimately be relied upon only when they remain in the state's interests to enforce.[3] Iran's commitments are no more or less trustworthy than were those of the Soviets, which is to say that agreements with Iran warrant adherence to the Reagan principle applied to the Soviets of "Trust but Verify."

One aspect of negotiating with Iran that poses particular difficulty is the strong likelihood that any Iranian leader who makes a concession on any matter of significance will be attacked domestically. We dealt with this problem in negotiations at The Hague by working on sets of claims advanced by each party, so that cases could be settled in a process that could not effectively be attacked as one-sided. In addition, we avoided formal agreements or understandings on sensitive matters. Discussions about the *fatwa* ordering the killing of Salman Rushdie, for example, led to an informal understanding that the *fatwa* would be treated as unenforceable outside Iran. That understanding was as good as any formal treaty, as long as it represented Iran's actual intent. Informal understandings enable Iranian negotiators to take steps without appearing to have capitulated to some US demand. Once a process of reconciliation is underway, greater openness and formality will become possible, and the parties will be able to address matters and make commitments that require formal arrangements.

A strategy for dealing with Iran based on increased strength and enhanced diplomacy will require a fundamental reset of US/Iranian relations. But that sort of shift will be familiar to anyone experienced in successful diplomacy. The United States knows how to stand up to a serious threat and how to negotiate effectively, as it demonstrated during the Cold War. Taking Iran seriously means treating it as a sovereign state whose excesses must actually be confronted, not merely wished away with threats of regime change, preventive war, and a crude and wildly fluctuating diplomacy instead of the sound methods used in US/Soviet relations.

One cannot be certain that a strategy of strength and diplomacy will ultimately succeed in convincing Iran to abandon its effort to develop nuclear weapons. But given the difficulties and dangers of undertaking preventive attacks on the facilities involved in producing them, and the need in any event to defend against IRGC aggression, it makes sense for the United States to seek to alter Iran's conduct through increased strength and more effective diplomacy, while leaving the preventive military option available if all else fails. In sum, the United States must get tougher with the IRGC and smarter with Iran.

Notes

Foreword

1. Secretary George P. Shultz, testimony before the Senate Foreign Relations Committee, *The Future of American Foreign Policy: New Realities and New Ways of Thinking*, 99th Congress, 1st session, 1985. (Current Policy No. 650, US Dept. of State Publication.)

Introduction

1. "The P5+1, Iran and the Perils of Nuclear Brinkmanship," International Crisis Group, June 15, 2012, accessed November 17, 2012, http://www.crisisgroup.org/~/media/Files/Middle%20East%20 North%20Africa/Iran%20Gulf/Iran/b034-the-p5-plus-1-iran-and-the -perils-of-nuclear-brinkmanship.

2. "Iran Will Not Relinquish One Iota of its Nuclear Rights: Ahmadinejad," *Tehran Times*, April 13, 2012, http://tehrantimes.com/ politics/96873-iran-will-not-relinquish-one-iota-of-its-nuclear-rights -ahmadinejad.

Chapter One

1. Barack Obama, "State of the Union Address,"Washington, DC, January 24, 2012. The White House, office of the press secretary, accessed November 20, 2012, http://www.whitehouse.gov/the-press-office/ 2012/01/24/remarks-president-state-union-address.

2. Nicolas Sarkozy, Speech to the Knesset (Israel, June 23, 2008) ("As far as France is concerned, a nuclear Iran is totally unacceptable."),

in Rebecca A. Stohl, "French President: Nuclear Iran is Totally Unacceptable," *The Jerusalem Post*, June 23, 2008, accessed January 10, 2013, http://www.jpost.com/Israel/Article.aspx?id=105237.

3. Angela Merkel, Speech at the 45th Munich Security Conference, (German transcript, Munich Security Conference, Munich, Germany, July 2, 2009), accessed November 20, 2012, http://www.securityconference.de/Dr-Angela-Merkel.216+M52087573ab0.0.html. Speech available in English at http://www.bundesregierung.de/statisch/nato/Content/EN/Reden/2009/2009–02–07-rede-merkel-sicherheitskonferenz-en_layoutVariant-Druckansicht.html.

4. Benjamin Netanyahu, "Netanyahu's Speech at AIPAC (full text)," *The Times of Israel*, March 6, 2012, accessed January 10, 2013, http://www.timesofisrael.com/netanyahus-speech-at-aipac-full-text/.

5. Leon Panetta, interview by Scott Pelley, on *60 Minutes*, CBS-TV, December 19, 2011, accessed November 11, 2012, http://www.cbsnews.com/2102–18560_162–57448437.html.

6. Ibid.

7. "President Obama's State of the Union Address," *New York Times*, January 25, 2012, accessed January 10, 2013, http://www.nytimes.com/interactive/2012/01/24/us/politics/state-of-the-union-2012-video-transcript.html.

8. Steven Holmes, "Clinton Warns North Korea Against Building Atom Bomb," *New York Times*, November 8, 1993, accessed November 20, 2012, http://www.nytimes.com/1993/11/08/world/clinton-warns-north-korea-against-building-atom-bomb.html.

9. Deborah Cameron, "North Korea Under Fire from All Sides," *Sydney Morning Herald*, October 6, 2006, accessed November 20, 2012, http://www.smh.com.au/news/world/north-korea-under-fire-from-all-sides/2006/10/05/1159641462765.html?from=rss.

10. Zbigniew Brzezinski and Robert M. Gates, *Iran: Time for a New Approach* (Washington, DC: Council on Foreign Relations, 2004), 13, www.cfr.org/content/publications/attachments/Iran_TF.pdf.

11. Guy Dinmore, "US Dismisses Any Thought of Thaw in Relations with Iran," *Financial Times*, February 14–15, 2004, 4; Scott Sagan, "How to Keep the Bomb From Iran," *Foreign Affairs* 85, no. 5 (September/October 2006), 45, 59; Flynt Leverett and Hillary Mann Leverett, "How to Defuse Iran," *New York Times*, December 11, 2007, A33, accessed January 10, 2013, http://www.nytimes.com/2007/12/11/opinion/11leverett.html?pagewanted=all&_r=0.

12. Dore Gold, *The Rise of Nuclear Iran: How Tehran Defies the West* (Washington, DC: Regnery Publishing, 2009), 309. Gold argues that the

best possible outcome would be for the Iranian people to overthrow the Islamic regime, and that the United States should support such an outcome by expressing its solidarity with opponents of the regime.

13. Shireen T. Hunter, "Post-Khomeini Iran," *Foreign Affairs* 68, no. 5 (Winter 1989/1990), 138.

14. The Iran Freedom Support Act (P.L. 109–293), September 30, 2006, 109th Congress, authorized "sums as may be necessary" to assist Iranians who support "democratic values . . . and the adoption of a democratic form of government in Iran. . . ."

15. Gold, *The Rise*, 307.

16. Peter David, "The Revolution Strikes Back: A Special Report on Iran," *The Economist*, July 21, 2007, 15–6, reporting on polls that show discontent with the economy but "do not prove . . . that Iran is ripe for counter-revolution." Israel's premier expert on Iran, Uri Lubrani, continues to predict the downfall of the Islamic regime, but now believes regime change is "not going to happen at this point. . . ." What he advocates—that the United States and others give their full support by "legal means" to those seeking freedom in Iran—is more like the effort proposed by Hassig and Oh regarding North Korea, i.e., to convince the Iranian people over time that their own government is their worst enemy.; David Horovitz, "Playing Chess Against Iran," *The International Jerusalem Post*, March 18–24, 2011, 10–3; Ralph C. Hassig and Kongdan Oh, "Prospects for Ending North Korea's Nuclear Weapons Program," *Foreign Policy Research Institute*, October 19, 2006, 8.

17. See, for example, Guy Dinmore and Najmeh Bozorgmehr, "Rumsfeld Pushes for Iran Action," *Financial Times*, May 30, 2003, 1, quoting Flynt Leverett, who served as senior director for Middle East affairs at the National Security Council and who has consistently contended that "the Iranians who used Ashura to make a political protest do not represent anything close to a majority." Flynt Leverett and Hillary Mann Leverett, "Another Iranian Revolution? Not Likely," *New York Times*, January 6, 2010, A20. Amir Taheri is hardly serious when he defines regime change as meaning that the United States should unalterably oppose and never accommodate Iran's ultimate objectives, but then recognizes the need and propriety to engage on specific issues including the nuclear program. The United States engaged with the Soviet Union without ever accepting that revolutionary regime or its ultimate objectives beyond treating it as a sovereign entity with which diplomacy had to be conducted. See his article, "Getting Serious About Iran: For Regime Change," *Commentary* (November 2006), 21, accessed January 10, 2013, http://www.commentary

magazine.com/article/getting-serious-about-iran-for-regime-change/.

18. Mark Mazzetti, "In '97, U.S. Panel Predicted a North Korea Collapse in 5 Years," *New York Times*, International Edition, October 27, 2006, A6.

19. Daniel C. Sneider, "North Korea: 4 Failures, 2 Dangers, 1 Opportunity: Is a United Response Possible?" *San Jose Mercury News*, October 15, 2006, 1.

20. Ray Takeyh, "A Profile in Defiance," *The National Interest* (Spring 2006), 16, 20–1, accessed January 10, 2013, http://nationalinterest.org/article/a-profile-in-defiance-1082.

21. Henry A. Kissinger, "A Nuclear Test for Diplomacy," *Washington Post*, May 16, 2006, accessed November 20, 2012, http://www.washingtonpost.com/wp-dyn/content/article/2006/05/15/AR2006051501200.html.

22. Sagan, "How to Keep," 53–54.

23. Elaine Sciolino, "United States and Europe Differ Over Strategy on Iran," *New York Times*, January 29, 2005, A3.

24. For an overview of the Security Council's sanctions against Iran, "UN Sanctions Against Iran," BBC News, Middle East, July 26, 2010, accessed January 11, 2013, http://www.bbc.co.uk/news/world-middle-east-10768146.

25. Benoit Faucon, "Sanctions Start to Hit Iranian Oil Shipping to Asia," *Wall Street Journal*, February 29, 2012, 6.

26. Council of the European Union, press release, *Iran: New EU Sanctions Target Sources of Finance for Nuclear Programme*, 3142th Foreign Affairs Council meeting (Brussels, January 23, 2012), 1, accessed November 20, 2012, http://www.consilium.europa.eu/uedocs/cms_data/docs/pressdata/EN/foraff/127444.pdf.

27. The White House, Executive Order: *Blocking Property of the Government of Iran and Iranian Financial Institutions*, February 6, 2012, accessed January 11, 2013, http://www.whitehouse.gov/the-press-office/2012/02/06/executive-order-blocking-property-government-iran-and-iranian-financial-.

28. Society for Worldwide Interbank Financial Telecommunication, press release, Simon Bale, "SWIFT Instructed to Disconnect Sanctioned Iranian Banks Following EU Council Decision," March 15, 2012, accessed January 11, 2013, http://www.swift.com/news/press_releases/SWIFT_disconnect_Iranian_banks.

29. Kenneth Katzman, *The Iran-Libya Sanctions Act*, Congressional Research Service (CRS), CRS Report RS20871, Office of Congressional

Publishing, August 8, 2006, accessed November 20, 2012, http://www
.dtic.mil/cgi-bin/GetTRDoc?AD=ADA475550.

30. Rick Gladstone, "India Explores Economic Opportunities in
Iran, Denting Western Sanctions Plan," *New York Times* International
Edition, February 10, 2012, A7; Pankaj Mishra, "Why India Goes Its
Own Way on Iran's Nuclear Program," Bloomberg, February 26, 2012,
accessed January 11, 2013, http://www.bloomberg.com/news/2012,
-02-27/india-goes-its-own-way-on-iran-s-nuclear-program-pankaj
-mishra.html.

31. Peter Enav, "US Bid to Crimp Iranian Oil Sales to Asia Stumbles,"
Bloomberg Businessweek, February 15, 2012, accessed November 20, 2012,
http://www.businessweek.com/ap/financialnews/D9STLIL02.htm.

32. Japan is particularly vulnerable, since it stopped relying on
nuclear power after the 2011 earthquake and tsunami severely damaged the Fukujima nuclear facility. Nuclear power had provided some
30 percent of the country's energy needs, and unless it comes back
online, power shortages seem likely, even if Iranian oil is used. See
"Nuclear Power in Japan," World Nuclear Association, May 2012,
accessed January 11, 2013, http://www.world-nuclear.org/info/inf79.
html; Osamu Tsukimori and Stanley White, "Japan May Cut Iran Oil
Imports by Over 20 Percent," Reuters, February 23, 2012, accessed January 11, 2013, http://www.reuters.com/article/2012/02/23/us-japan
-usa-sanctions-idUSTRE81L28L20120223.

33. On February 19, 2012, Iran's oil ministry announced that it
would halt shipments to Britain and France ahead of the European
Union's oil embargo, which was set to begin in July. See Joby Warrick,
"Iran Halts Oil Shipments to Britain, France," *Washington Post*, February
19, 2012, accessed January 11, 2013, http://www.washingtonpost.com/
world/middle_east/iran-halts-oil-shipments-to-britain-france/
2012/02/19/gIQAnLtUNR_story.html.

34. Otto Reich and Ezequiel Vazquez Ger, "Iran's Stealth Financial
Partners in Latin America," *Miami Herald*, March 14, 2012, accessed
January 11, 2013, http://www.opeal.net/index.php?option=com_k2&
view=item&id=10518:iran%E2%80%99s-stealth-financial-partners
-in-latin-america&Itemid=142; Benoit Faucon and Margaret Coker,
"Obscure Banks Plug Gap in Iran," *Wall Street Journal*, April 9, 2012, C1;
Matthew Rosenberg and Annie Lowrey, "Iranian Currency Traders
Find a Haven in Afghanistan," *New York Times*, August 17, 2012, A4,
accessed January 11, 2013, http://www.nytimes.com/2012/08/18/
world/middleeast/iranian-currency-flows-into-afghanistan-markets
.html?pagewanted=all.

35. Dmitry Zhdannikov and Justyna Pawlak, "Britain Seeks Delay to EU's Iran Ship Insurance Ban," Reuters, May 9, 2012, accessed November 12, 2012, http://www.reuters.com/article/2012/05/09/us-iran-eu -insurance-idUSBRE84806K20120509.

36. Stanley J. Marcuss and George F. Murphy, "Alert: The New U.S. Sanctions Against Iran," *California International Law Journal* (Fall 2011): 35.

37. Kenneth Katzman, *Iran Sanctions* (CRS 2012), Congressional Research Service (CRS), Office of Congressional Publishing, December 7, 2012, accessed January 11, 2013, http://www.cfr.org/iran/crs-iran -sanctions/p28272, summary & 50. The report notes several significant limitations in the coverage of UN sanctions (p. 37), as well as ways in which India (by means of barter), China and Turkey (gold), Tanzania (reflagging vessels), and others have helped Iran avoid their impact (pp. 41–4).

38. Meir Dagan et al., "Total Sanctions Might Stop Iran," *Wall Street Journal*, May 17, 2012, A15.

39. Dennis B. Ross, "Iran is Ready to Talk," *New York Times*, February 14, 2012, A25, accessed January 11, 2013, http://www.nytimes.com/ 2012/02/15/opinion/give-diplomacy-with-iran-a-chance.html.

40. David Feith, "What Obama Isn't Saying About Iran," *Wall Street Journal*, August 17, 2012, A11. According to Feith, the volume of oil exports is stabilizing, and the government has an estimated $60 billion to $100 billion in foreign currency reserves. He notes that all of Iran's major oil-trading partners have received exemptions from the oil embargo, and that China, India, and other major trading partners generally continue to do business with Iran.

41. Sagan, "How to Keep," 46.

42. Steven Erlanger, "Europe Takes Bold Step Toward a Ban on Iranian Oil," *New York Times*, January 4, 2012, accessed November 20, 2012, http://www.nytimes.com/2012/01/05/world/europe/europe-moves -toward-ban-on-iran-oil.html?pagewanted=all.

43. Helene Cooper, "Sanctions Against Iran Grow Tighter, but What's the Next Step?" *New York Times* European edition, January 25, 2012, A4, quoting Vali Nasr: "These latest sanctions are weakening the regime, but they're also putting pressure on the regime, which is arriving to the point where the Iranians have no motivation other than to get their nuclear capabilities faster."

44. "Iran Primer," usip.org/blog/2012/oct/11/west-claims-sanctions.

45. Rebecca Lowe, "Iran: from prince to pariah," *IBA Global Insight* (June 2012), 25.

46. Gold, *The Rise*, 923–43; Wyn Q. Bowen and Jonathan Brewer, "Iran's Nuclear Challenge: Nine Years and Counting," *International Affairs* 87, no. 4 (2011).

47. Ray Takeyh, "All the Ayatollah's Men," *The National Interest* (September/October 2012), 51 (Takeyh writes, "A narrow segment of the conservative clerical elite, commanding key institutions of the state, has fashioned a foreign policy designed to maintain the ideological character of the regime.").

48. Gold, *The Rise*, 307, 17.

49. Ibid., 269. See also Joshua Muravchik and Jeffrey Gedmin, "Why Iran Is (Still) a Menace," *Commentary*, July 1997, 39–44, a typical critique of the sort of "engagement" the US has thus far attempted with Iran (including the appeal leading to the Iran/Contra Affair).

50. James Dobbins et al., *"Coping with a Nuclearizing Iran,"* RAND *Corporation*, (2009), 88–104, accessed November 20, 2012, http://www.rand.org/pubs/monographs/MG1154.html.

51. "Weighing Benefits and Costs of Military Action Against Iran," *Wilson Center* (2012), http://www.wilsoncenter.org/sites/default/files/IranReport_091112_FINAL.pdf. (The report is endorsed by a number of distinguished former diplomats, and provides valuable guidance on the consequences of preventive military actions.)

52. Sense of the Senate resolution, 112th Cong. 2nd sess. (2012): MDM12140, http://freebeacon.com/wp-content//uploads/2012/02/MDM12140.pdf.

53. Helene Cooper, "'Loose Talk of War' Only Helps Iran, President Says," *New York Times*, March 4, 2012, accessed November 11, 2012, http://www.nytimes.com/2012/03/05/world/middleeast/in-aipac-speech-obama-warns-against-loose-talk-of-war.html.

54. Bret Stephens, "(How) Should Israel Bomb Iran?" *Wall Street Journal*, February 7, 2012, accessed November 20, 2012, http://online.wsj.com/article/SB10001424052970204369404577206943198066220.html.

55. "Israel Must be Eliminated," *Wall Street Journal* editorial, September 26, 2016, A18. The statements have been condemned by UN Secretary General Ban Ki Moon as "offensive and inflamatory." "U.N. chief condemns Iran leaders' anti-Israel remarks," August 7, 2012, accessed November 20, 2012, http://articles.chicagotribune.com/2012–08–17/news/sns-rt-us-Iran-Israel_anti-Israel-remarks-supreme-leader-attack-Iranian-nuclear-facilities.

56. Gold, *The Rise*, 292–4; Scott Peterson, "Waiting for the Rapture in Iran," *Christian Science Monitor*, December 21, 2005, accessed November 20, 2012, http://www.csmonitor.com/2005/1221/p01s04-wome.html; Bret Stephens, "Iran Cannot Be Contained," *Commentary* (July/August 2010), 61. Former President Akbar Rafsanjani's less explicit but

chilling analysis is often cited. He notes that a nuclear exchange with Israel would destroy the Jewish state but "will only harm the Islamic world."

57. Benjamin Netanyahu, Speech to the American Israel Public Affairs Committee, Washington, D.C. (March 5, 2012).

58. David Lev, "Saudi FM: Iran is 'A Threat to the Entire Middle East'," *Arutz Sheva*, November 24, 2011, accessed November 20, 2012, http://www.israelnationalnews.com/News/News.aspx/150067# .T76ZgL 8xNxk.

59. Kissinger, "A Nuclear Test "; Ron Tira, "Can Iran be Deterred," *Policy Review* (October/November 2011): 39. The author uses game theory to demonstrate how much more complex it would become to manage nuclear proliferation in the Middle East if Iran becomes nuclear armed than it was between the Soviet Union and the US during the Cold War.

60. David E. Sanger and Thom Shanker, "Response to Nuclear Threats Hinges on Policy Debate," *New York Times*, May 8, 2007, A9.

61. For example, the former Israeli military intelligence chief, Major General (res.) Amos Yadlin, has said that "a nuclear-armed Iran is more dangerous than attacking Iran," adding: "If they can't be contained, when they don't have nuclear weapon[s], how can they be contained when they do?" Quoted in Natasha Morgovaya, "Ex-IDF Intelligence Chief: A Nuclear Iran is More Dangerous than Military Strike," *Haaretz*, May 5, 2012, 1.

62. Tobias Buck, "Israel Warns Tehran Soon Immune to Attack," *Financial Times*, February 2, 2012, 3.

63. John Bolton, "Iran's Assassination Plot Compels a Tough Response," *The Guardian*, October 21, 2011, accessed November 20, 2012, http://www.guardian.co.uk/commentisfree/cifamerica/2011/oct/21/ iran-assassination-plot.

64. Edward N. Luttwak, "The President Has Been Given A False Choice on Iran," *Wall Street Journal*, February 18–19, 2012, A13. Luttwak has written, however, that as of 2006 Iran had demonstrated incompetence in putting together a nuclear weapon and that no rush existed to use force at that time. Edward N. Luttwak, "Three Reasons Not to Bomb Iran—Yet," *Commentary* (May 2006): 21 (". . . the regime is still years away from producing a bomb." Luttwak also cites the long-term consequences of any US military action as a reason to delay and if possible avoid bombing Iran—for example, to keep open the possibility of its again becoming a US ally).

65. Brent J. Talbot, "Stuxnet and After," *Journal of International Security Affairs* 69, no. 21 (Fall/Winter 2011) (Israeli Vice Prime Minister Moshe Yaalon claimed that no Iranian facility is safe from Israeli attacks, and that, while Iran may need about a year to complete a bomb, an attack will become impractical months sooner). Nathan Podhoretz, "The Case for Bombing Iran," *Commentary* (June 2007), accessed November 20, 2012, http://www.commentarymagazine.com/article/the-case-for-bombing-iran/.

66. Podhoretz, "The Case," 17, 21; Norman Podhoretz, "Stopping Iran: Why the Case for Military Action Still Stands," *Commentary* (February 2008), 11. Podhoretz Senior was responding to the National Intelligence Estimate's 2007 assessment that it was uncertain whether Iran currently intended to develop nuclear weapons. US agencies continue to adhere to the position that Iran has not yet moved to build a nuclear weapon. James Risen and Mark Mazzetti, "U.S. Agencies See No Move by Iran to Build a Bomb," *New York Times*, February 25, 2012, 1.

67. Arnold Beichman, "Ramping Up On Iran," *Washington Times*, March 18, 2007.

68. "Reading Israel on Iran," *International Jerusalem Post*, week of July 20–26, 2012, 16. The article asks whether Israeli and US threats regarding Iran are a "bluff," as suggested by *Time* magazine.

69. Israeli Defense Minister Ehud Barak in "Israel Says Threat of Strike on Iran is Working," *Agence France Press*, March 23, 2012, accessed from Yahoo News, November 20, 2012, http://www.rawstory.com/rs/2012/03/22/israel-says-threat-of-strike-on-iran-is-working/; Ethan Bronner, "When Talk of War Transcends Idle Chatter," *New York Times*, February 6, 2012, A10.

70. David E. Sanger, "U.S and North Korea Reach Nuclear Deal," *New York Times*, September 3, 2007, A5. Soon thereafter, North Korea withdrew its offer.

71. Colin Robinson and Stephen H. Baker, "Stand-off with North Korea: War Scenarios and Consequences," *Center for Defense Information*, accessed November 20, 2012, http://openscenarios.ida.org/scenarios/270-Stand-off_with_North_Korea.pdf.

72. Harry S. Truman, *Memoirs, Vol. II: Years of Trial and Hope* (Garden City, NY: Doubleday, 1956), 383.

73. National Security Council, *NSC 68: United States Objectives and Programs for National Security*. A Report to the President Pursuant to The President's Directive of January 31, 1950, April 14, 1950, http://www.fas.org/irp/offdocs/nsc-hst/nsc-68–9.htm, accessed November 20, 2012.

74. "Top secret" memo from President Dwight Eisenhower, to Secretary of State John Foster Dulles, September 8, 1953, in *The Papers of Dwight David Eisenhower*, ed. L. Galambos and D. van Ee, doc. 404. World Wide Web facsimile by The Dwight D. Eisenhower Memorial Commission of the print edition; Baltimore, MD: The Johns Hopkins University Press, 1996, http://www.eisenhowermemorial.org/presidential-papers/first-term/documents/404.cfm.

75. Marc Trachtenberg, "A Wasting Asset: American Strategy and the Shifting Nuclear Balance, 1949–1954," *International Security* 13, no. 3 (Winter 1988/89), 40.

76. Basic National Security Policy, *Foreign Relations of the United States, 1952–1954*, (Washington, DC: U.S. Government Printing Office, 1975), VII, Part 1, 815, December 14, 1954, http://digital.library.wisc.edu/1711.dl/FRUS.FRUS195254v02p1, accessed November 20, 2012.

77. Jeffrey Record, "Nuclear Deterrence, Preventive War, and Counterproliferation," *Policy Analysis, Cato Institute*, no. 519, July 8, 2004, 15, http://www.cato.org/pubs/pas/pa519.pdf, accessed November 20, 2012.

78. Richard K. Betts, "The Osirak Fallacy," *The National Interest* (Spring 2006): 22.

79. "Iran's Key Nuclear Sites," *BBC New Middle East*, January 9, 2012, accessed November 11, 2012, http://www.bbc.co.uk/news/world-middle-east-11927720.

80. Kori Schake, "Dealing with a Nuclear Iran," *Policy Review* (April/May 2007): 3.

81. "Rethinking Our Approach to Iran's Search for the Bomb," *Center for Strategic and International Studies*, May 7, 2012, 1–2, http://csis.org/print/37079.

82. Various sets of demands or proposals have been advanced by government officials and commentators from the US, Europe, Israel, Iran, Turkey, Brazil, and elsewhere. As proposed by US Senators Lindsay Graham, Joseph I. Lieberman, and John McCain ("Getting a Good Deal With Iran," *Wall Street Journal*, May 23, 2012, A15), the ultimate objective, generally stated, would be to have Iran agree to abandon—in a verifiable manner—its pursuit of nuclear-weapons capabilities. See also Prime Minister Netanyahu's publicly stated demands that "Iran must stop all enrichment of nuclear material; it must remove all materials enriched to date from its territory; and it must dismantle its underground nuclear enrichment plant at Qom." In addition, see Herb Keinon, "In Obama We Trust?" *Jerusalem Post*, June 1, 2012, 13.

83. E.g., David Crawford and Jay Solomon, "U.N. Atomic Chief Tries Tehran Gambit," *Wall Street Journal*, May 19–20, A6.

84. Mark Fitzpatrick, "Consider the Consequences: A Pre-emptive Attack on Iran Would be an Act of Folly," *Security Times* (Special Edition of the *Atlantic Times*, issued for the 48th Munich Security Conference), February 2, 2012; Fitzpatrick argues that a preemptive attack on Iran's nuclear facilities would be an act of folly. Some speculate that Iran is using North Korea as a base for nuclear work. In November 2006, Iran's and North Korea's nuclear collaboration increased. Con Coughlin, "North Korea Helping Iran with Nuclear Testing," *The (London) Telegraph*, January 24, 2007, accessed November 20, 2012. In January 2007, a senior European defense official told the *Telegraph*, "North Korea had invited a team of Iranian nuclear scientists to study the results of last October's underground test to assist Teheran's preparations to conduct its own." These reports are based on blog postings by Green Correspondents of Iran, as stated in "Iranian Regime Seeks North Korea's Help to Activate Ballistic Missiles," trans.). Green Correspondents of Iran, "Iranian Regime Seeks North Korea's Help to Activate Ballistic Missiles," trans. Utkanos, *CNN iReport*, December 10, 2011, accessed November 20, 2012, http://ireport.cnn.com/docs/DOC-715823.

85. Anonymous, "Retired General: U.S. Can Live with a Nuclear Iran," *CNN World*, September 18, 2007, accessed November 20, 2012, http://articles.cnn.com/2007–09–18/world/france.iran_1_nuclear -weapon-nuclear-program-nuclear-fuel?_s=PM:WORLD (referring to the views of General John Abizaid, former US commanding general in Iraq.

86. Paul Richter, "Gates Warns Against Israeli Strike on Iran's Nuclear Facilities," *Los Angeles Times*, April 16, 2009, accessed November 20, 2012, http://articles.latimes.com/2009/apr/16/world/fg-us -iran16.

87. CNN Wire Staff, "Gates: Sanctions are Impacting Iran," *CNN World*, November 8, 2010, accessed November 20, 2012, http://articles .cnn.com/2010-11-08/world/iran.us.options_1_nuclear-program -foreign-minister-manouchehr-mottaki-sets-of-un-sanctions? _s=PM:WORLD.

88. Secretary Leon Panetta, speech, "Remarks by Secretary of Defense Leon E. Panetta at the Saban Center," Washington, DC, http:// www.defense.gov/transcripts/transcript.aspx?transcriptid=4937; Thom Shanker, Helene Cooper, and Ethan Bronner, "U.S. Sees Iran Attacks as Likely if Israel Strikes," *New York Times*, February 29, 2012, accessed November 20, 2012, http://www.nytimes.com/2012/02/29/ world/middleeast/us-sees-iran-attacks-as-likely-if-israel-strikes .html?pagewanted=all. (In this article, the former chairman of the Joint

Chiefs of Staff, General James E. Cartwright, is quoted as saying that Iran's reaction to an attack would most likely be to strike a balance that inflicts significant damage but is "just short of what it would take for America to invade.") US war games indicate that "it may be impossible to preclude American involvement in any escalating confrontation with Iran. . . ." Mark Mazzetti and Thom Shanker, "U.S. War Game Sees Perils of Israeli Strike Against Iran," *New York Times*, March 19, 2012, accessed November 20, 2012, http://www.nytimes.com/2012/03/20/world/middleeast/united-states-war-game-sees-dire-results-of-an-israeli-attack-on-iran.html?pagewanted=all; Carl Bildt and Erkki Tuomioja, "The Only Option on Iran," *New York Times,* March 21, 2012, accessed November 20, 2012, http://www.nytimes.com/2012/03/21/opinion/the-only-option-on-iran.html?ref=iran.

89. Schake, "Dealing with," 19–20. Even if Iran were to acquire nuclear weapons, Schake proposes that a variety of military options would exist, including attacks after warning of "an Iranian nuclear use," given the time and distinctive activities a nuclear attack by Iran would require.

90. U.S. Department of Defense, Missile Defense Agency, "Joint U.S.-Israel Arrow Weapon System Intercepts Target During Successful Missile Defense Test," *Missile Defense Agency News Release*, February 22, 2011, http://www.mda.mil/news/11news0002.html; Thom Shanker, "U.S. and Gulf Allies Pursue a Missile Shield Against Iranian Attack," *New York Times*, August 9, 2012, A9.

91. Colin H. Kahl, "Not Time to Attack Iran: Why War Should Be a Last Resort," *Foreign Affairs*, March/April 2012, p. 166; James M. Lindsay and Ray Takeyh, "After Iran Gets the Bomb: Containment and Its Complications," *Foreign Affairs* (March/April 2010), 42–9, accessed November 20, 2012, http://www.foreignaffairs.com/articles/66032/james-m-lindsay-and-ray-takeyh/after-iran-gets-the-bomb; Lyn E. Davis, et al., *Iran's Nuclear Future: Critical U.S. Policy Choices* (Santa Monica, CA: RAND Corporation, 2011), http://www.rand.org/pubs/monographs/MG1087.

92. Fareed Zakaria, "How History Lessons Could Deter Iranian Aggression," *Washington Post*, February 15, 2012, accessed November 20, 2012, http://www.washingtonpost.com/opinions/history-could-be-a-deterrent-to-iranian-aggression/2012/02/15/gIQA6UVcGR_story.html.

93. Yossi Melman, "Former Mossad Chief: Israel Air Strike on Iran 'Stupidest Thing I Have Ever Heard'," *Haaretz*, May 7, 2011, accessed November 20, 2012, http://www.haaretz.com/news/diplomacy

-defense/former-mossad-chief-israel-air-strike-on-iran-stupidest-thing
-i-have-ever-heard-1.360367.

94. Ilan Evyatar, "The Art of Espionage," *Jerusalem Post*, April 5, 2012, accessed November 20, 2012, http://www.jpost.com/Features/ MagazineFeatures/Article.aspx?id=265000.

95. Abdullah Toukan and Anthony Cordesman, "Study on a Possible Israeli Strike on Iran's Nuclear Development Facilities," *Center for Strategic and International Studies*, March 14, 2009, 4, accessed November 20, 2012, http://csis.org/files/media/csis/pubs/090316_israelis trikeiran.pdf.

96. Former Israeli Prime Minister Ehud Olmert said to Christiane Amanpour: "Whatever may happen in Iran, all the assessments made by all the intelligence agencies that I've heard—and I've heard them all—is that Iran will react and that may trigger a regional war in the Middle East which would impact the stability of the Middle East, the economic situation, which will have far-reaching consequences on many different countries, and which may cause a terrible damage to the status of Israel, the economic situation of Israel, to the political status of Israel and whatnot. And I'm not certain that this is the last resort. "Christiane Amanpour, interview with Ehud Olmert," *CNN*, April 30, 2012, accessed November 20, 2012, http://transcripts.cnn.com/TRANSCRIPTS/1204/ 30/ampr.01.html.

97. John Rudoren, "Ex-Security Chief Says Israeli Government is 'Misleading' Public About Iran," *New York Times*, April 29, 2012, 10; Isabel Kershner, "Israel's President Criticizes Talk of Unilateral Strike on Iran," *New York Times*, August 17, 2012, A3.

98. Leslie Susser, "Spy Vs. Spy," *Jerusalem Report*, March 26, 2012, 6. This article summarizes the arguments and personalities on both sides of the debate within Israel over whether to attack Iran's nuclear program.

99. Tobias Buck, "Israel Warns on Iran Immunity from Attack," *Trove* 3 (National Library of Australia), http://trove.nla.gov.au/work/162094 033?versionId=176653085.

100. Ethan Bronner, "Israelis Assess Threats by Iran As Partly Bluff," *New York Times*, January 27, 2012, 1.

101. Buck, "Israel Warns," 3. Buck says: "The world today has no doubt that the Iranian military nuclear programme is slowly but surely reaching the final stages, and will enter the immunity stage from which point the Iranian regime will be able to complete the programme without any effective intervention and at its convenience."

102. Amos Yadlin, "Israel's Last Chance to Strike Iran," *New York Times*, February 29, 2012, A27; Jeffrey Goldberg, "The Point of No

Return," *The Atlantic* (September 2010): 56. General Martin Dempsey, Chairman US Joint Chiefs of Staff, agrees that the US and Israel have different "clocks," but predicts that an Israeli attack could only delay, not destroy, Iran's nuclear project. "US, Israel view Iran threat with different 'clocks': general," *Google News*, August 19, 2012, accessed November 20, 2012, http://www.google.com/hostednews/afp/article/ALeqM5gw13qR3rjfBEe2ywYWecqyzCHvaA.

103. Agence France Presse, "Analysis: Pre-emptive Strike Talk Keeps Israel's Iran Options Open," *Taipei Times*, February 10, 2012, accessed November 20, 2012, http://www.taipeitimes.com/News/world/archives/2012/02/10/2003525152.

104. See Carol E. Lee and Jay Solomon, "Obama Shifts Toward Israel on Iran," *Wall Street Journal*, March 5, 2012, A7; Mark Landler, "Obama Says Option to Strike Iran Not a 'Bluff,' but Cites Repercussions," *New York Times*, March 3, 2012, A4; Mark Landler, Thom Shanker, and Helene Cooper, "A Hard Line on Iran Places the Administration in a Bind," *New York Times*, March 30, 2012, A10. US Ambassador to Israel, Dan Shapiro, took the process of extending assurances to Israel even further on May 17, 2012, when he said at an Israel Bar Association meeting that the option of military force against Iran is "not just available, but it's ready. The necessary planning has been done to ensure that it's ready." Jodi Rudoren, "U.S. Envoy to Israel Says Nation is Ready on Iran," *New York Times*, May 18, 2012, A5.

105. Daniel Levy, "Netanyahu Won't Attack Iran," *New America Foundation*, March 2, 2012, accessed November 20, 2012, http://www.newamerica.net/publicatns/articles/2012/netanyahu_wont_attack_eiran_64983.

106. Landler et al., "A Hard Line": "The concern about going to war with Iran that is emanating from the Pentagon did not start with Defense Secretary Leon E. Panetta. His predecessor, Robert M. Gates, as well as Adm. Mike Mullen, the former chairman of the Joint Chiefs of Staff, were equally outspoken. 'Both of those guys were counseling on the risks of military action, and quite publicly,' said a senior military official. 'Their successors have reaffirmed that—and that is where the building's leadership is on this.'"

107. An analysis of the relevant considerations that concludes in favor of attempting containment is provided by Justin Logan, *The Bottom Line on Iran: The Costs and Benefits of Preventive War versus Deterrence*, Policy Analysis Paper No. 583 (Washington, DC: Cato Institute), December 4, 2006.

108. See Iran Project Report, "Timing, Objectives, Capabilities and Exit Strategy for Military Action." Weighing Benefits and Costs of Military Action Against Iran. The Iran Project, September 11, 2012, http://www.wilsoncenter.org/sites/default/files/IranReport_091112_FINAL.pdf.

Chapter Two

1. George W. Bush, "Blocking Property of Weapons of Mass Destruction Proliferators and Their Supporters," Executive Order 13382, June 28, 2005, accessed November 20, 2012, http://www.state.gov/t/isn/c22080.htm#dprk.

2. U.S. Department of Treasury (DoT), Office of Foreign Assets Control, *Specially Designated Nationals and Blocked Persons,* updated April 23, 2012, accessed December 21, 2012, http://www.treasury.gov/ofac/downloads/t11sdn.pdf.

3. Frederic Wehrey, et al., *The Rise of the Pasadran: Assessing the Domestic Roles of Iran's Islamic Revolutionary Guards Corps,* (Santa Monica, CA: RAND Corporation, 2009); Edward N. Luttwak, "Three Reasons Not to Bomb Iran—Yet," *Commentary* (May 2006), 21–3. See also the concise but useful description of the Iranian Revolutionary Guard Corps (IRGC) in Tal Becker, *Terrorism and the State* (Portland, OR: Hart Publishing, 2006), 242–3.

4. James Dobbins, Sarah Harting, and Dalia Dassa Kaye, *Coping with Iran: Confrontation, Containment, or Engagement? A Conference Report* (Santa Monica, CA: RAND Corporation, 2007), 14, 20–4; Bret Stephens, "Iran's Al Qaeda," *Wall Street Journal,* October 16, 2007, A20. For a concise and informative description of the IRGC, see Stratfor, *The Islamic Revolutionary Guard Corps,* Parts 1 & 2, October 26, 2012, which concludes that "Were the IRGC to weaken, so too would the regime."

5. Kenneth M. Pollack, *The Persian Puzzle: The Conflict Between Iran and America* (New York: Random House, 2004), 290.

6. Dalal Saoud, "Khatami Warns U.S. Against 'Other Crises'," *UPI.com,* May 13, 2003, 1.

7. *Interpretative Declaration of Iran for the Convention Against the Taking of Hostages, 1979,* November 20, 2006, accessed November 20, 2012, http://www.adh-geneva.ch/RULAC/international_treaties.php?id_state=109http://www.adh-geneva.ch/RULAC/Treaty_List.pdf. Iran asserts, as an exception to the hostage convention, that "fighting terrorism should not affect the legitimate struggle of peoples under colonial

domination and foreign occupation in the exercise of their right of self-determination."

8. Abbas Milani, "Khosrow Ruzbeh," in *Eminent Persians* (Syracuse, NY: Syracuse University Press, 2008), 277: "In their [Shiite] epistemology; their vision of truth, logic, and style of textual exegesis; their organizational commitment to vanguards and hierarchy; their messianic sense of history and mechanistic aesthetics that places art completely in the service of dogma; their advocacy of 'just war' and 'revolutionary' violence; their belief in social engineering and the necessity of creating a 'new man'; and their view of the individual and society as 'instruments' of some higher purpose, they tap into the same craving for certainty, and for human agency, that is at once individual and collective. They are both equally dismissive of the kind of ambiguities about truth and human nature that are at the core of a democratic polity. Both claim the mantle of 'true science'—one had Stalin's infamous 'dialectical materialism' in mind when it talked of science, and the other has long claimed access to nothing less than the infinite wisdom of God. No wonder, then, that while mullahs have long called themselves ulama, or men of science, in postwar Iran the 'scientific method' became a non-too-oblique metaphor for Marxism."

9. Pollack, *The Persian Puzzle*, 201.

10. "Terrorist Attacks on Americans, 1979–1988," *Frontline*, Public Broadcasting System (PBS), accessed November 20, 2012, http://www.pbs.org/wgbh/pages/frontline/shows/target/etc/cron.html.

11. Charles Waterman, "Islamic Jihad-hostage-takers with an Iranian connection," *Christian Science Monitor*, June 17, 1985.

12. Bob Woodward and Charles R. Babcock, "Captive CIA Agent's Death Galvanized Hostage Search; Buckley's Plight became Agency Crusade," *Washington Post*, November 25, 1986.

13. Bob Woodward, "Exclusive Excerpts from 'VEIL'; The Secret Wars of the CIA," *Newsweek*, October 5, 1987.

14. *Brewer v. Islamic Republic of Iran*, 664 F. Supp. 2d 43 (DC Cir. 2009), accessed November 20, 2012, http://docs.justia.com/cases/federal/district-courts/district-of-columbia/dcdce/1:2008cv00534/130417/20/0.pdf.

15. Ibid., 13.

16. Ibid., 14.

17. Jeffrey Goldberg, "A Reporter At Large: In the Party of God (Part II): Hezbollah Sets Up Operations in South America and the United States," *The New Yorker*, October 28, 2002, accessed November

20, 2012, http://www.jeffreygoldberg.net/articles/tny/a_reporter_at _large_in_the_par_1.php.

18. Ibid.

19. George P. Shultz, *Turmoil and Triumph: My Years as Secretary of State* (New York: Scribner, 1993), 665.

20. Elisabeth Smick, "Profile: Imad Mugniyah," *Council on Foreign Relations Study*, February 13, 2008, accessed November 20, 2012, http://www.cfr.org/iran/profile-imad-mugniyah/p11317#p9.

21. Goldberg, "A Reporter at Large," 4.

22. Ronen Bergman, *The Secret War with Iran: The 30-Year Clandestine Struggle Against the World's Most Dangerous Terrorist Power* (New York: Free Press, 2008), 67.

23. Ibid., 241.

24. Hala Jaber, *Hezbollah: Born with a Vengeance* (New York: Columbia University Press, 1997), 119.

25. Jaber, *Hezbollah*, 117.

26. Kenneth Katzman, *Iran's Influence in Iraq*, CRS, Report RS73938, September 29, 2006, http://fpc.state.gov/documents/organization/73938.pdf.

27. Kenneth Katzman, *Iran-Iraq Relations*, CRS, Report RS22323, August 13, 2010, accessed November 20, 2012, http://www.fas.org/sgp/crs/mideast/RS22323.pdf.

28. Ibid., 2.

29. Ibid., 4.

30. Ed O'Keefe and Joby Warrick, "Weapons Prove Iranian Role in Iraq, U.S. says," *Washington Post*, July 5, 2011, accessed November 17, 2012, http://www.washingtonpost.com/world/war-zones/weapons -prove-iranian-role-in-iraq-us-says/2011/07/05/gHQAUnkmzH _story.html.

31. Julian Barnes, "Mullen Accuses Tehran of Arming Iraq Militias," *Wall Street Journal*, July 8, 2011, accessed November 20, 2012, http://online.wsj.com/article/SB10001424052702304793504576432312 376139394.html.

32. "U.S. Concerned Iran Providing Weapons to Iraq Militants," Reuters in *Haaretz*, July 11, 2011, accessed November 20, 2012, http://www.haaretz.com/news/middle-east/u-s-concerned-iran -providing-weapons-to-iraq-militants-1.372670.

33. Jim Garamone, "Extremists Use Iranian Weapons, Iraq Command Spokesman Says," *American Forces Press Service*, July 11, 2011, accessed November 20, 2012, http://www.defense.gov/news/news article.aspx?id=64630.

34. Ed O'Keefe and Joby Warrick, "Weapons Prove Iranian Role in Iraq, U.S. says," *Washington Post,* July 5, 2011, accessed January 23, 2013, http://articles.washingtonpost.com/2011–07–05/world/35237463 _1_kataib-hezbollah-weapons-shiite-militia-groups.

35. See, for example, Joseph Felter and Brian Fishman, "Iranian Strategy in Iraq: Politics and Other Means," Combating Terrorism Center at US Military Academy, West Point, October 13, 2008, 55–70, accessed November 20, 2012, http://www.ctc.usma.edu/wp-content/uploads/2010/06/Iranian-Strategy-in-Iraq.pdf.

36. Michael R. Gordon and Bernard E. Trainor, *The Endgame: The Inside Story of the Struggle for Iraq, From George W. Bush to Barack Obama,* (New York: Random House, 2012), 319. The authors write: "The United States never used the intelligence it gathered to strike training camps or EFP factories in Iran."

37. Michael R. Gordon, "Iran's Master of Iraq Chaos Still Vexes U.S.," *New York Times,* October 2, 2012, accessed November 20, 2012, http://www.nytimes.com/2012/10/03/world/middleeast/qassim -suleimani-irans-master-of-iraq-chaos-still-vexes-the-us.html.

38. Martin Chulov, "Qais al-Khazali: from kidnapper and prisoner to potential leader," *The Guardian,* December 31, 2009, accessed November 20, 2012, http://www.guardian.co.uk/world/2009/dec/31/iran -hostages-qais-al-khazali.

39. Ali A. Nabhan and Julian E. Barnes, "Iraq Frees Militant Wanted in Deaths of U.S. Soldiers, *Wall Street Journal,* November 17–8, 2012, A10.

40. Suadad al-Salhy, "Iraqi militia threatens U.S. interest over film," *Reuters,* September 13, 2012, accessed November 20, 2012, http://www .reuters.com/article/2012/09/13/us-iraq-usa-threat-idUSBRE88 C0CK20120913.

41. Report, "Hizb-i-islami Gulbuddin (HIG)," Institute for the Study of War (2007–2012), Washington, DC, http://www.understandingwar .org/hizb-i-islami-gulbuddin-hig.

42. Clay Wilson, *Improvised Explosive Devices (IEDs) in Iraq and Afghanistan: Effects and Countermeasures,* CRS Report RS22330, August 28, 2007, accessed November 20, 2012, http://www.fas.org/sgp/crs/weapons/RS22330.pdf.

43. Associated Press (AP), "Iranian-made Rockets Seized in Afghanistan," *Navy Times,* March 9, 2011, accessed November 20, 2012, http://www.navytimes.com/news/2011/03/ap-iranian-rockets -seized-in-afghanistan-030911/.

44. Jay Solomon, "Iran Funnels New Weapons To Iraq and Afghanistan," *Wall Street Journal,* July 2, 2011, accessed November 20, 2012,

http://online.wsj.com/article/SB100014240527023037634045764200 80640167182.html.

45. Editorial, "White House Admits War with Iran," *Washington Times*, July 14, 2011, accessed November 20, 2012, http://www.washington times.com/news/2011/jul/14/white-house-admits-war-with-iran/.

46. Sanjeev Miglani, "General McChrystal Says Afghan Insurgents Trained in Iran," Reuters, May 30, 2010, accessed November 20, 2012, http://www.*reuters*.com/article/2010/05/30/us-afghanistan-iran -idUSTRE64T0U920100530.

47. U.S. Department of Treasury press release, "Fact Sheet: U.S. Treasury Department Targets Iran's Support for Terrorism, Treasury Announces New Sanctions Against Iran's Islamic Revolutionary Guard Corps–Qods Force Leadership," August 3, 2010, accessed November 20, 2012, http://www.treasury.gov/press-center/press-releases/Pages/ tg 810.aspx.

48. U.S. Department of Treasury press release, "Treasury Targets Key Al-Qa'ida Funding and Support Network Using Iran as a Critical Transit Point," July 28, 2011, http://www.treasury.gov/press-center/ press-releases/Pages/tg1261.aspx.

49. Ibid.

50. David Feith, "The Warrior's-Eye View of Afghanistan," *Wall Street Journal*, May 12–13, 2012, A33.

51. Federal Bureau of Investigation (FBI), press release, "Khobar Towers Indictment," June 21, 2001, accessed November 20, 2012, http:// www.au.af.mil/au/awc/awcgate/khobar/khobar_fbi.htm.

52. *United States v. Al-Mughassil* (Khobar Towers indictment), US District Ct, Eastern Dist of VA, Alexandria Div., June 2001, accessed November 20, 2012, http://www.au.af.mil/au/awc/awcgate/khobar/ khobar_indictment.pdf.

53. In May 1998, *The New York Times* reported that Prince Nayef bin Abdul Aziz, head of Saudi ministry of interior, claimed "No foreign party had any role in it." In June 2007, Secretary of Defense William Perry blamed Osama bin Laden for the bombing, stating that the Saudis were anxious to divert attention elsewhere due to potential US retaliation. See "Perry: U.S. Eyed Attack After Bombing," *United Press International*, June 6, 2007. In *Khobar Towers Investigated* (2009), Gareth Porter questions the validity of admissions obtained during torture. He notes that al-Qaeda sought to target US interests in Saudi Arabia, that a Saudi cover-up would redirect the US response to the bombing, and that FBI Director Louis Freeh's personal relationship with Saudi Ambassador Prince Bandar bin Sultan, which eventually led to his serving as

Bandar's attorney, helped position Freeh to blame the Iranians. However, even National Security Advisor Sandy Berger, who was unhappy to be presented with evidence indicating Iranian involvement, agreed that the Iranians were involved, claiming only that the extent of their involvement was unknown until late 1999. President Clinton does not address what he calls the "dangerous" issue of determining whether Iran was responsible.

54. The evidence of IRGC involvement, based on the FBI's investigation and testimony in court is summarized in *Rimkus v. The Islamic Republic of Iran*, 750 F. Supp. 2d 163 (Dist. Ct Dist. of Columbia 2010), accessed January 22, 2013, http://scholar.google.com/scholar_case?case=547418466808453374&hl=en&as_sdt=2&as_vis=1&oi=scholarr.

55. United Nations Security Council Resolution 457, December 4, 1979, S/RES 45; United Nations Security Council Resolution 461, December 31, 1979, S/RES 457; Order of the International Court of Justice, December 15, 1979, S/13697. The ICJ found that, although the original act of taking over the embassy was not attributable to Iran (because the militants were not acting on the government's behalf), the government failed to observe its obligations to protect the staff under the 1961 Vienna Convention on Diplomatic Relations and the 1963 Vienna Convention on Consular Relations. Khomeini's subsequent vocal support of the militants, moreover, made them agents of Iran, making the ensuing hostage crisis attributable to Iran. United States Diplomatic and Consular Staff in Tehran (*Iran v. U.S.A.*), 1980 International Court of Justice, May 24, 1980). See analysis in Bernard Lewis, "The Revolt of Islam," *The New Yorker*, November 19, 2001, accessed November 20, 2012, http://www.newyorker.com/archive/2001/11/19/011119fa_FACT2#ixzz1vofT0Xt4. As Lewis notes, "One of the most surprising revelations in the memoirs of those who held the American Embassy in Teheran from 1979 to 1981 was that their original intention had been to hold the building and the hostages for only a few days. They changed their minds when statements from Washington made it clear that there was no danger of serious action against them. They finally released the hostages, they explained, only because they feared that the new president, Ronald Reagan, might approach the problem "like a cowboy."

56. *U.S. v. Usama Bin Laden*, S(6) 98 Cr. 1023 (LBS), (2nd Cir. 1998), 6, accessed November 20, 2012, http://www.fas.org/irp/news/1998/11/indict1.pdf.

57. The 9/11 Commission, *Final Report of the National Commission on Terrorist Attacks Upon the United States*, official government edition (Washington, DC: U.S. Government Printing Office, 2004), 61.

58. Peter Finn, "Al Qaeda Deputies Harbored by Iran," *Washington Post*, August 27, 2002, A01.

59. Ibid.

60. Clint Watts, Jacob Shapiro, and Vahid Brown, *Al-Qaida's (Mis) Adventures in the Horn of Africa* (West Point, NY: Harmony Project, Combating Terrorism Center, Department of Social Sciences, US Military Academy, July 2007), 124, accessed January 22, 2013, http://www.ctc.usma.edu/posts/al-qaidas-misadventures-in-the-horn-of-africa.

61. Ibid., 124–5.

62. Report, *Terrorism 2002–2005*, December 9, 2007 (Federal Bureau of Investigation, US Department of Justice), accessed November 20, 2012, http://www.fbi.gov/stats-services/publications/terrorism-2002 –2005.

63. Pollack, *The Persian Puzzle*, 358–61.

64. U.S. Department of State, "Delisting of the Mujahedin-e Khalq," September 28, 2012, accessed November 20, 2012, http://www.state.gov/r/pa/prs/ps/2012/09/198443.htm.

65. Con Coughlin, "Iran Receives Al Qaeda Praise for Role in Terrorist Attacks," *Telegraph*, November 23, 2008, accessed November 20, 2012, http://www.telegraph.co.uk/news/worldnews/middleeast/iran/3506544/Iran-receives-al-Qaeda-praise-for-role-in-terrorist -attacks.html.

66. Helene Cooper, "Treasury Accuses Iran of Aiding Al Qaeda," *New York Times*, July 28, 2011, accessed November 20, 2012, http://www.nytimes.com/2011/07/29/world/29terror.html.

67. Department of Treasury, press release, "Treasury Targets Key Al-Qa'ida Funding and Support Network Using Iran as a Critical Transit Point," July 28, 2011, accessed November 20, 2012, http://www.treasury.gov/press-center/press-releases/Pages/tg1261.aspx.

68. "Al-Rahman is al-Qa'ida's overall commander in Pakistan's tribal areas." *Id.*, http://www.treasury.gov/press-center/press-releases/Pages/tg 1261.aspx.

69. "WikiLeaks Exposé: Saudis Told U.S. 'Cut Off the Head of the Snake,' on Iran," Reuters in *Haaretz*, November 29, 2012, accessed November 20, 2012, http://www.haaretz.com/news/world/wikileaks -expose-saudis-told-u-s-cut-off-the-head-of-the-snake-on-iran -1.327502.

70. "Salehi Dismisses US Claim of Iran's Plotting Against Saudi, Zionist Embassies," *Arabs Today*, October 13, 2011, accessed November 17, 2012, http://www.arabtoday.net/index.php?option=com_content &view=article&id=42704&catid=208&Itemid=84.

71. Benjamin Weiner, "Man Pleads Guilty in Plot to Murder Saudi Envoy," *New York Times*, October 18, 2012, A24.

72. Iran Human Rights Documentation Center, *No Safe Haven: Iran's Global Assassination Campaign* (New Haven, CT: 2008), 67–76.

73. Department of Treasury, press release, "Treasury Sanctions Five Individuals Tied to Iranian Plot to Assassinate the Saudi Ambassador to the United States," October 11, 2011, accessed November 20, 2012, http://www.treasury.gov/press-center/press-releases/pages/tg1320. aspx. The decision states in part: "Designated today pursuant to Executive Order (E.O.) 13224 for acting for or on behalf of the IRGC-QF were: Manssor Arbabsiar, a naturalized U.S. citizen holding both Iranian and U.S. passports who acted on behalf of the IRGC-QF to pursue the failed plot to assassinate the Saudi ambassador; IRGC-QF commander Qasem Soleimani; Hamed Abdollahi, a senior IRGC-QF official who coordinated aspects of the plot and oversaw the other Qods Force officials directly responsible for coordinating and planning this operation; Abdul Reza Shahlai, an IRGC-QF official who coordinated this operation; and Ali Gholam Shakuri, an IRGC-QF official and deputy to Shahlai, who met with Arbabsiar on several occasions to discuss the assassination and other planned attacks."

74. Peter Finn, "Notorious Iranian Militant has a Connection to Alleged Assassination Plot Against Saudi Envoy," *Washington Post*, October 14, 2011, accessed November 20, 2012, http://www.washingtonpost .com/world/national-security/notorious-iranian-militant-has-a-con nection-to-alleged-assassination-plot-against-saudi-envoy/2011/ 10/14/gIQAJ3E6kL_story.html.

75. Parisa Hafezi and Jeremy Pelofsky, "Washington Says Iran Sought Killing of Saudi Envoy," *Reuters*, October 12, 2011, accessed November 20, 2012, http://www.reuters.com/article/2011/10/12/us -usa-security-iran-newspro-idUSTRE79B4YA20111012.

76. Tony Capaccio and John Walcott, "Iran Stepping Up Spying, Support for Terror, Clapper Says," *Bloomberg News Service*, January 31, 2012; Siobhan Gorman, "Spy Chief Sees Iran Threats in U.S.," *Wall Street Journal*, February 1, 2012, A8.

77. Pollack, *The Persian Puzzle*, 214.

78. Former Iranian Intelligence officer Abolghassem Mesbahi defected and testified in the German-restaurant slaying trial that Iran's leadership had a list of 500 "enemies of Islam," drawn up by the Ayatollah Khomeini, who were targeted for elimination. By 1996, several dozen of them had been killed, pursuant to decisions made by a select group called the Committee of Special Operations. The restaurant vic-

tims had appeared on Khomeini's list of dissidents who had fled Iran. Even before the Mikanos Restaurant killings, hundreds of individuals on the list were murdered in locations as widespread as Austria and Japan. Report, "No Safe Haven: Iran's Global Assassination Campaign," Iran Human Rights Documentation Center (New Haven; IHRDC 2008).

79. As summarized in "Vom Attentat bis zum Ricterspruch," on *Welt Online*, the assassins were arrested in late 1993, creating tension between Germany and Iran. In October 1993, Iran's intellegence minister, Hajatoleslam Ali Fallahian, went to Bonn to try to convince the Germans to stop the trial, but failed. Iran threatened adverse consequences to its relations with Germany if the alleged ringleader, Kazem Darabi, were convicted. Chancellor Kohl and President Rafsanjani issued condemnatory statements, and some Iranian clergy issued death threats against German prosecutors. In 1996, the German trial court found that Iran's secret service planned the attack and sent the assassins to Berlin. In April 1997, the court convicted all four suspects and formally attributed responsibility for the killings to Iran's leadership, which it found had acted for the purpose of liquidating the Kurdish dissident party. After the sentencing, Germany recalled its ambassador from Tehran; Iran recalled several members of its delegation from Germany. Darabi and Rhayel received life sentences with no eligibility for parole for at least 23 years; their two accomplices were sentenced to 11 and five-plus years, respectively. Darabi and Rhayel were released in 2007, however, on the grounds that German law allows the early release of prisoners who are immediately deported; the decision may have been related to the release by Iran six months earlier of a German fisherman who had been imprisoned for 16 months after his boat crossed accidentally into a restricted zone in the Persian Gulf. "Drahtzieher des Mykonos-Attentats Freigelssen," *Welt Online*, October 12, 2007.

80. Ibid., 268.

81. Karim Sadjadpour in Bernard Gwertzman, "Iran Supports Hamas, but Hamas Is No Iranian 'Puppet'," Council on Foreign Relations, January 8, 2009, accessed November 20, 2012, http://www.cfr.org/israel/iran-supports-hamas-but-hamas-no-iranian-puppet/p18159.

82. Israel Ministry of Foreign Affairs, Press Release, "Seizing of the Palestinian Weapons Ship Karine A," January 3, 2002, accessed January 22, 2013, http://www.mfa.gov.il/MFA/Government/Communiques/2002/Seizing%20of%20the%20Palestinian%20weapons%20ship%20Karine%20A%20-.

83. Centre for Israel and Jewish Affairs, "Inside Report: IDF Discovery of Deadly Anti-Ship Missiles En Route to Gaza," March 24, 2011,

accessed November 20, 2012, http://www.cicweb.ca/scene/2011/03/inside-report-idf-discovery-of-deadly-anti-ship-missiles-en-route-to-gaza/.

84. Aaron Klein, "Iran Supplies Hezbollah with 3,000 More Rockets: Shipment Enough to Fire into Israel at Current Rate for Additional Month," *WorldNetDaily*, July 26, 2006, accessed November 20, 2012, http://www.wnd.com/?pageId=37213.

85. Steven Emerson and Joel Himelfarb, "Would Iran Provide a Nuclear Weapon to Terrorists?," *inFocus Quarterly*, Winter 3, no. 4 (2009), 3, accessed November 20, 2012, http://www.jewishpolicycenter.org/1532/iran-nuclear-weapon-to-terrorists.

86. United Nations Security Council, *Summary Report of the 6090th Meeting*, official record, S/PV.6090 (New York, March 10, 2009), accessed November 20, 2012, http://www.securitycouncilreport.org/atf/cf/%7B65BFCF9B-6D27-4E9C-8CD3-CF6E4FF96FF9%7D/Iran%20S%20PV%206090.pdf.

87. Ibid.

88. Anthony H. Cordesman, "Iran's Revolutionary Guards, the Al Quds Force, and Other Intelligence and Paramilitary Forces," Center for Strategic and International Studies, August 16, 2007: 10.

89. Lieutenant Colonel (ret.) Michael Segall, "Does Iran's Latest Military Exercise Signal a New Defense Doctrine?" (blog), Jerusalem Center for Public Affairs, July 6, 2011, accessed November 20, 2012, http://jcpa.org/does-iran%E2%80%99s-latest-military-exercise-sign al-a-new-defense-doctrine/.

90. "Iran Charged over Argentina Bomb," *BBC News*, October 26, 2006, accessed November 20, 2012, http://news.bbc.co.uk/2/hi/6085768.stm.

91. Marc A. Thiessen, "Iran Responsible for 1998 U.S. Embassy Bombings," *Washington Post*, December 8, 2011, accessed November 20, 2012, http://www.washingtonpost.com/opinions/iran-responsible-for-1998-us-embassy-bombings/2011/12/08/gIQAuEAAfO_story.html.

92. "Key Suspect in the Bombing of an Istanbul Synagogue Arrested," *Los Angeles Times*, November 30, 2003, accessed November 20, 2012, http://articles.latimes.com/2003/nov/30/world/fg-turkey30.

93. See the discussion in Chapter 3.

94. Admiral James A. Lyons (Ret.), "Only One Solution to Iran: Regime Change; With Hostile Forces Soon Off Our Coast, Support for Opposition is Crucial," *Washington Times*, October 6, 2011, B4, accessed November 20, 2012, http://www.washingtontimes.com/news/2011/

oct/6/only-one-solution-to-iran-regime-change/. The Pentagon has filmed video of Iranian harrassment of US vessels, which Iran has claimed are fake. Nazila Fathi, "Iran Accuses U.S. of Faking Video of Boat Showdown in Gulf," *New York Times,* January 10, 2008, A14.

95. J. David Goodman, "Iran Warns U.S. Aircraft Carrier Not to Return to Gulf and a Strategic Strait." *New York Times,* January 3, 2012, accessed November 20, 2012, http://www.nytimes.com/2012/01/04/world/middleeast/iran-warns-the-united-states-over-aircraft-carrier.html?_r=1; Editorial, Iran's Hormuz Threat," *Wall Street Journal,* December 30, 2011, A14, accessed November 20, 2012 (Iran's "threat is another opportunity to set boundaries on Iran's rogue behavior.").

96. Secretary Leon Panetta and General Martin Dempsey, interview by Bob Schieffer, *Face the Nation,* CBS News, January 8, 2012, transcript, accessed November 20, 2012, http://www.cbsnews.com/8301-3460_162-57354647/face-the-nation-transcript-january-8-2012/.

97. Thom Shanker and Ride Gladstone, "Iran Fired on Military Drone in First Such Attack, U.S. Says," *New York Times,* November 8, 2012, accessed November 20, 2012, http://www.nytimes.com/2012/11/09/world/middleeast/pentagon-says-iran-fired-at-surveillance-drone-last-week.html?pagewanted=all&_r=0.

Chapter Three

1. Charles Krauthammer, "The Reagan Doctrine," Essay, *Time,* April 1, 1985, http://www.time.com/time/magazine/article/0,9171,964873,00.html.

2. Leonid Brezhnev, "Brezhnev Doctrine: Speech by First Secretary of the Soviet Union Leonid Brezhnev," International Relations and Security Network, November 13, 1968, accessed November 20, 2012, http://www.rohan.sdsu.edu/dept/polsciwb/brianl/docs/1968BrezhnevDoctrine.pdf.

3. In President Carter's January 23, 1980, State of the Union address, he said, "Let our position be absolutely clear: An attempt by any outside force to gain control of the Persian Gulf region will be regarded as an assault on the vital interests of the United States of America, and such an assault will be repelled by any means necessary, including military force. "

4. President J. Carter, "Jimmy Carter: The President's News Conference," November 28, 1979, The American Presidency Project, accessed November 20, 2012, http://www.presidency.ucsb.edu/ws/index.php?pid=31752#axzz1ni VcL2eH.

5. Jimmy Carter to Ayatollah Khomeini, November 6, 1979, accessed November 20, 2012, http://www.archives.gov/historical-docs/doc-content/images/carter-letter-iran-hostages.pdf.

6. James Holloway, *The Holloway Report*, Joint Chiefs of Staff, August 23, 1980, accessed November 20, 2012, http://www.gwu.edu/~nsarchiv/NSAEBB/NSAEBB63/doc8.pdf. (The plan called for eight helicopters to fly six hundred miles from the USS *Nimitz* to Tehran in tight formation at low altitude, with no lights and no radio communication. See Pollack, *The Persian Puzzle*, 169. *The Holloway Report* attributed the failure to deficiencies in mission planning, command and control, and inter-service operability.

7. Pollack, *The Persian Puzzle*, 254.

8. Peter W. Rodman, *Presidential Command* (New York: Alfred A. Knopf, 2009), 130. For additional insight into the failed helicopter mission, and other useful analysis of Carter's weak handling of foreign affairs, see William J. Bennett, *America: The Last Best Hope, Vol. II* (Nashville, TN: Thomas Nelson, 2007), 470, quoting Carter's National Security Adviser, Zbigniew Brzezinski, saying that the Carter Administration's members tended to "shy away from the unavoidable ingredient of force in dealing with contemporary realities, and to have an excessive faith that all issues can be resolved by compromises" and to "equate foreign policy with endless litigation and to confuse détente with acquiescence."

9. Gold, *The Rise*, 86–91.

10. Shultz, *Turmoil and Triumph*, 230.

11. Pollack, *The Persian Puzzle*, 205.

12. Shultz, *Turmoil and Triumph*, 231.

13. See Gold, *The Rise*, 92.

14. Bernard Gwertzman, "McFarlane Took Cake and Bible to Teheran, Ex-C.I.A. Man Says," *New York Times*, January 11, 1987, accessed November 17, 2012, http://www.nytimes.com/1987/01/11/us/mcfarlane-took-cake-and-bible-to-teheran-ex-cia-man-says.html?pagewanted=all&src=pm.

15. "The Iran-Contra Affair," *The American Experience*, accessed November 20, 2012, http://www.pbs.org/wgbh/americanexperience/features/general-article/reagan-iran/.

16. Michael White, "Iran Invites US to Admit it Needs Improved Relations: Rafsanjani Says Links Are in American Interest," *The Guardian* (London), December 20, 1986.

17. "Iran," *Foreign Broadcast Information Service (FBIS)*, Middle East & South Asia Review, November 5, 1986, 1. On November 28, 1986, Rafsanjani said: "Our principles have been the same from the begin-

ning. Today too we say that if the Americans will stop bullying and will return our assets which have been confiscated in the United States, then from this podium we shall ask the Lebanese people to assist you in the problem of the hostages." "Friday Prayers View U.S. 'Crisis,' Hostages," *FBIS*, LD291216, Tehran Domestic Service in Persian, 11.

18. "Is U.S. Going to Change its Policy?," Opinion, *FBIS*, December 23, 1986, 2; "Hashemi Rafsanjani Urges Release of Frozen Assets," *FBIS*, LD191746, Tehran IRNA in English, December 19, 1986: "Rafsanjani said here Friday that once the U.S. Government should release the entirety of Iranian assets in the U.S. banks and elsewhere; the Islamic Government would then intercede with the Shi'ite groups in Lebanon for the release of the American hostages in that country."

19. "Majlis Speaker on U.S. Attempts To Resume Ties," *FBIS*, LD271501 Tehran IRNA, in English, February 28, 1987, 11–12.

20. Robert J. McCartney, "Rafsanjani: Relations Turn on U.S. Policy," *Washington Post*, April 21, 1987, A21.

21. Pollack, *The Persian Puzzle*, 227.

22. Ibid., 231.

23. Daniel Crist, *The Twilight War: The Secret History of America's Thirty-Year Conflict with Iran* (New York: Penguin Press, 2012), 356–7. Crist summarizes the damage done to the Iranians during Operation Praying Mantis, including 60 killed and over 100 wounded, and notes that the attacks of April 18, 1988, "greatly reduced the Iranian navy as a major threat to tanker traffic." He quotes the emir of Bahrain as telling an American commander: "The Iranians don't understand anything but power. . . . Next time give it to them one thousand times harder!")

24. E.g., Nora Boustany, "Iranians Offer Help On Hostages if Assets Would be Released; White House Refuses to Link Frozen Funds, Western Captives," *Washington Post*, August 9, 1989, A1.

25. Walter S. Mossberg, "U.S. Will Return $567 Million Total in Iranian Assets," *Wall Street Journal*, November 7, 1989, A4; AP, "U.S. Agrees to Return $567 Million to Iran," *Washington Post*, November 7, 1989, A14; Richard Lacayo, William Dowell, and Jay Peterzell, "A Game of Winks and Nods," *Time*, November 20, 1989, 39.

26. George H.W. Bush, "George Bush: The President's News Conference," The American Presidency Project, November 7, 1989, accessed November 20, 2012, http://www.presidency.ucsb.edu/ws/index.php ?pid=17762#ax zz1xmu6GA4q.

27. AP, "Paper Says Recent Release of Assets Not Enough 'Goodwill'," *Moscow-Pullman Daily News*, November 9, 1989, 2A.

28. "Magazine Cited on Iranian-U.S. Claims Settlements," *FBIS*, FBIS-NES-90-027, LDO702142590, Tehran IRNA, in English, February 7, 1990, 58.

29. Don Oberdorfer, "Iran Paid for Release of Hostages," *Washington Post*, January 19, 1992, A1. An editorial in the *Tehran Times* on February 22, 1990, stated, for example, that "all forces active in the Lebanon scene must make efforts to help free all hostages from whatever nationality they might be. The release of hostages is an Islamic, ethical and humanitarian move." "Hostages in Lebanon Are Victims of Western Hegemony," *FBIS*, FBIS-NES-90-040, NC2802074090, *Tehran Times*, in English, February 28, 1990, 2. Hezbollah's spiritual leader, Mohamad Hussein Fadlallah, was reported on February 25, 1990, as saying: "We should find practical and humanitarian ways to free the foreign hostages because this issue is being heavily exploited by the Westerners to present a bad picture of Islam and the Muslims." "Hostage Issue U.S. Propaganda Tool," Editorial, *FBIS*, FBIS-NES-90-043, NC0503120090, Tehran ETTELA'AT, in Persian, February 25, 1990, 2.

30. Thomas L. Friedman, "U.S. and Iran in Accord on 2,500 Small Claims," *New York Times*, May 10, 1990, A6.

31. Abraham D. Sofaer, "No Quick Fix in Iran," *Washington* Post (1990), A11, partial article link: http://www.highbeam.com/doc/1P2 -1136377.html.

32. Gold, *The Rise.*

33. Don Oberdorfer, "Diplomacy Steps From Shadows; Talks Take on Official Trappings, Air for General Release of Captives," *Washington Post*, August 28, 1991, A1; Nora Boustany, "Cleric Says Iran Wants Hostage Issue Resolved," *Washington Post*, August 9, 1991, A1. Rafsanjani reportedly replaced a radical Hezbollah leader, Subhi Tufaili, with a more moderate one, Abbas Musawi, in order to facilitate the hostage release he wanted to achieve. See, Caryle Murphy, "Financial and Political Factors Seen Adding Pressure on Captors, Iranians, Lebanese Dropping Support for Kidnappers, Diplomats Say," *Washington Post*, August 10, 1991, A18.

34. Elaine Sciolino, "The Last U.S. Hostage," *New York Times*, December 6, 1991, A1.

35. Don Oberdorfer, "Iran Paid for Release of Hostages," *Washington Post*, January 19, 1992, 1.

36. E.g., William Claiborne, "Iran Pledges to Aid U.N. on Hostages; Rafsanjani, Perez de Cuellar Seem Hopeful After Israeli Action," *Washington Post*, September 12, 1991, A26. Despite its efforts, Israel was unable to obtain information about its missing pilot, Ron Arad. Patrick E. Tyler,

"Talks on Hostages Have Bogged Down Over Israeli Flyer," *Washington Post*, September 8, 1991, 1. The hostage release ultimately proceeded without addressing this Israeli demand, as Hezbollah leader Abbas Musawi announced the issues would no longer be linked. See William Drozdiak, "Shift by Shiites Seen Speeding Release of Western Hostages," *Washington Post*, November 21, 1991, A44; Ihsan A. Hijazi, "Hostage Releases are Linked to U.N.," *New York Times*, December 4, 1991, A11.

37. Elaine Sciolino, "U.S. Near Deal to Settle Claims By the Iranians," *New York Times*, November 21, 1991, A1; Sciolino, "U.S. and Iran Sign a Compensation Pact," *New York Times*, November 28, 1991, A3.

38. William Claiborne, "U.S.-Iranian Cooperation Seen Possible," *Washington Post*, September 19, 1991, A39; William Drozdiak, "Hostages' Release Serves Iran's Goal of Larger Third World Role," *Washington Post*, November 19, 1991, A26.

39. Oberdorfer, "Iran Paid."

40. David Hoffman, "Many Obstacles Remain to Closer U.S.-Iran Ties," *Washington Post*, December 6, 1991, A39.

41. Chris Hedges, "Islamic Hard-Liners Said to Gain Ground in Iran," *New York Times*, August 3, 1994, A3.

42. Jeffrey Smith and Daniel Williams, "White House to Step Up Plans to Isolate Iran, Iraq; Administration to Try 'Dual Containment'," *Washington Post*, May 23, 1993, A26.

43. Martin Indyk, "The 'Dual Containment Speech': The Clinton Administration's Approach to the Middle East," *U.S.-Iranian Relations: An Analytic Compendium of U.S. Policies, Laws and Regulations*, The Atlantic Council of the United States, ed. Kenneth Katzman (Washington, DC: Atlantic Council, December 1999), 8, accessed November 20, 2012, http://carnegieendowment.org/pdf/npp/iranregulations.pdf.

44. New York Times News Service, "Administration making effort to isolate Iran Plan Seeks to Weaken Tehran," *Baltimore Sun*, May 27, 1993, accessed November 20, 2012, http://articles.baltimoresun.com/1993-05-27/news/1993147205_1_iran-nuclear-weapons-policy.

45. Suzanne Maloney, "Fear and Loathing in Tehran," *The National Interest* (Sept./Oct. 2007), 43, accessed November 20, 2012, http://www.brookings.edu/~/media/research/files/articles/2007/9/iran%20maloney/20070918.pdf. Maloney notes that, in February 1995, Speaker of the House Newt Gingrich, who originally pushed for the $18 million in the U.S. intelligence budget for covert activities, called for a strategy that was "ultimately designed to force the replacement of the current regime in Iran, which is the only long-range solution that makes any sense."

46. Pollack, *The Persian Puzzle*, 275.

47. Chris Hedges, "Iranians, Marking '79 Crisis, Assail U.S. as Rift Again Widens" *New York Times*, November 5, 1993, A7, accessed November 20, 2012, http://www.nytimes.com/1993/11/05/world/iranians-marking-79-crisis-assail-us-as-rift-again-widens.html.

48. Pollack, *The Persian Puzzle*, 276.

49. Ibid. See also, Anthony Bruno, "The Bombing of Khobar Towers," *truTV*, http://www.trutv.com/library/crime/terrorists_spies/terrorists/khobar_towers/3.html.

50. Pollack, *The Persian Puzzle*, 284–6.

51. Elaine Sciolino, "Criticized Over Iran's Strength, U.S. Struggles to Develop New Policy for Region," *New York Times*, April 20, 1977, p. 4.

52. "Praying Mantis was an unqualified success for the United States." Crist, *The Twilight War*, 356.

53. Ibid.

54. Bill Clinton, *My Life*, 717–8.

55. Christiane Amanpour, "Transcript of Interview with Iranian President Mohammad Khatami," *CNN*, January 7, 1998, accessed November 20, 2012, http://www.cnn.com/WORLD/9801/07/iran/interview.html.

56. Pollack, *The Persian Puzzle*, 315.

57. Ibid., 316–8.

58. Brian Knowlton, "Clinton Offers 'Genuine Reconciliation' to Iran," *New York Times*, June 19, 1998, http://www.nytimes.com/1998/06/19/news/19iht-iran.t_6.html.

59. Elaine Sciolino, "A Top Iranian Aide Rejects US Overture on New Ties," *New York Times*, September 29, 1998, accessed November 20, 2012, http://www.nytimes.com/1998/09/29/world/a-top-iranian-aide-rejects-us-overture-on-new-ties.html?pagewanted=2.

60. Knowlton, "Clinton Offers," accessed November 17, 2012, http://www.nytimes.com/1998/06/19/news/19iht-iran.t_6.html.

61. Pollack, *The Persian Puzzle*, 323–4.

62. Louis J. Freeh, "Khobar Towers," *Wall Street Journal*, June 23, 2006, A10, accessed November 20, 2012, http://www.iranvajahan.net/cgi-bin/news.pl?l=en&y=2006&m=06 &d=23&a=5.

63. Press release, "Terrorism Charges Have Been Brought Against 13 Members of the Pro-Iran Saudi Hizballah," FBI (Washington, DC), June 21, 2001, accessed November 20, 2012, http://www.fbi.gov/news/pressrel/press-releases/terrorism-charges-have-been-brought-against-13-members-of-the-pro-iran-saudi-hizballah.

64. Jamie Rubin, State Department Noon Briefing, US embassy, Tel Aviv, March 8, 2000, http://usembassyisrael.org.il/publish/peace/archives/2000/march/me0308d.html.

65. "Iran Seeks to End U.S. Trade Ban," Institute for Agriculture and Trade Policy, March 9, 2000, accessed November 17, 2012, http://www.iatp.org/news/iran-seeks-end-to-us-trade-ban.

66. "U.S. Moves to Improve Relations with Iran," Asia Society, accessed November 17, 2012, http://www.djc.com/news/tech/1100 5600.html.

67. Testimony of Michael Rubin, "Iran: Recent Developments and Implications for U.S. Policy," House Foreign Affairs Committee, July 22, 2009, accessed November 20, 2012, http://www.meforum.org/2409/iran-developments-implications-us-policy.

68. "Leader's Speech on the Day of Eid Ghadir at Mausoleum in Mashhad," Al-Hadj Library Website of Hadji Information, March 25, 2000, accessed November 20, 2012, http://www.al-hadj.com/html/en/library/6644/7.htm.

69. Lee H. Hamilton, James Schlesinger, and Brent Scowcroft, *Thinking Beyond the Stalemate in U.S.-Iranian Relations, Vol. 1*, (Washington, DC: The Atlantic Council of the United States, 2001), 3, accessed November 20, 2012, http://www.acus.org/files/publication_pdfs/82/0105-Thinking_Beyond_Stalemate_U.S._Iranian_Relations.pdf.

70. "Iran—Sept. 7—Khatami Says 'Serious Issues' Hamper US Meetings," *APS Diplomat Recorder*, September 9, 2000, accessed November 20, 2012, http://www.thefreelibrary.com/IRAN+-+Sept.+7+-+Khatami+Says+'Serious+Issues'+Hamper+US+Meetings.-a073739328.

71. Lionel Beehner, Backgrounder, Timeline: U.S.–Iran Contacts, Council on Foreign Relations, March 9, 2007, accessed February 1, 2013, http://www.cfr.org/iran/timeline-us-iran-contacts/p12806.

72. Freeh, "Khobar Towers."

73. Bruce O. Riedel, "The Iran Primer: The Clinton Administration," United States Institute of Peace, accessed November 20, 2012, http://iranprimer.usip.org/resource/clinton-administration.

74. *Iranian Response to Clinton Letter*, National Security Archive (Clinton Library; Clinton Presidential Records, 1999), accessed November 20, 2012, http://www.gwu.edu/~nsarchiv/NSAEBB/NSAEBB318/doc03.pdf.

75. "Khatami Says Sanctions Will Hurt the U.S. More than Iran," *Associated Press*, November 16, 2000, accessed November 20, 2012, http://www.farsinet.com/news/nov2000wk3.html.

76. Freeh, "Khobar Towers."

77. Gold, *The Rise*, 145. Gold presents valuable information on the conflict underway within the Iranian government at the time the Clinton Administration (and other states) were reaching out to Khatami for meaningful change. He notes that "Khatami's ability to influence [Major General Yahya Rahim Safavi, commander of the Revolutionary Guards] was virtually nil. . . . The West paid attention to Khatami, but not to the realities of Iranian policies that were being executed by Khamenei and by the Revolutionary Guards. No one wanted to take strong measures against Iran—and sustain them—for such action might undermine the reformist trend led by Khatami."

78. Andrew C. McCarthy, "Murder of U.S. Airmen at Khobar Towers: Iran Did It," *National Review Online*, December 22, 2006, accessed November 20, 2012, http://www.nationalreview.com/corner/135018/murder-us-airmen-khobar-towers-iran-did-it-andrew-c-mccarthy.

79. Barbara Slavin, *Bitter Friends, Bosom Enemies: Iran, the U.S., and the Twisted Path to Confrontation*, (New York: St. Martin's Griffin, 2009), 193–4.

80. Hillary Mann, "U.S. Diplomacy with Iran: The Limits of Tactical Engagement," Statement to the Subcommittee on National Security and Foreign Affairs Committee on Government Oversight and Reform, U.S. House of Representatives, November 7, 2007, 5, accessed November 20, 2012, http://democrats.oversight.house.gov/images/stories/subcommittees/NS_Subcommittee/11.7.07_Iran_II/HillaryMann Leveretttestimony1107.pdf.

81. Ibid.

82. Slavin, *Bitter Friends, Bosom Enemies*, 201.

83. James Dobbins, *After the Taliban: Nation Building in Afghanistan* (Dulles, Virginia: Potomac Books, 2008), 103.

84. Gold, *The Rise*, 154.

85. Sam Donaldson, interview with Secretary of Defense Donald Rumsfeld, *ABC This Week*, February 3, 2002, U.S. Department of Defense, accessed November 20, 2012, http://www.defense.gov/transcripts/transcript.aspx?transcriptid=2440.

86. Remarks by National Security Advisor Condoleezza Rice to the Conservative Political Action Conference, Arlington, Virginia, January 31, 2002, accessed November 20, 2012, http://www.usembassy-israel.org.il/publish/peace/archives/2002/february/020105.html.

87. Slavin, *Bitter Friends, Bosom Enemies*, 200.

88. Pollack, *The Persian Puzzle*, 353.

89. Mann, *US Diplomacy*, 7.

90. Barbara Slavin, "U.S., Iran holding talks in Geneva," *USA Today*, May 11, 2003, accessed November 20, 2012, http://www.usatoday.com/news/world/2003–05–11-iran-usat_x.htm.

91. Karen DeYoung, *Soldier: The Life of Colin Powell* (New York: Alfred A. Knopf, 2006), 462.

92. Gareth Porter, "Iran Proposal to U.S. Offered Peace with Israel," *Institute for Public Studies*, May 24, 2006, accessed November 20, 2012, http://www.ipsnews.net/2006/05/politics-iran-proposal-to-us-offered-peace-with-israel/.

93. DeYoung, *Soldier*, 462.

94. Michael Hirsh and Maziar Bahari, "Blowup? America's Hidden War with Iran," *Newsweek*, February 12, 2007.

95. Elaine Sciolino, "Europeans Say Iran Agrees to Freeze Uranium Enrichment," *New York Times*, November 16, 2004, A3.

96. Elaine Sciolino, "United States and Europe Differ Over Strategy on Iran," *New York Times*, January 29, 2005, A3.

97. Report, "History of Official Proposals on the Iranian Nuclear Issue," Arms Control Association, April 2012, accessed November 20, 2012, http://www.armscontrol.org/factsheets/Iran_Nuclear_Proposals.

98. Ronald E. Neumann, as quoted in Report, Mir H. Sadat and James P. Hughes, "US-Iran Engagement Through Afghanistan," Middle East Policy Council, 17, no. 1, 31–51, accessed November 20, 2012, http://mepc.org/journal/middle-east-policy-archives/us-iran-engagement-through-afghanistan.

99. Ibid.

100. Slavin, *Bitter Friends*, 218.

101. See Steven R. Weisman, "U.S. is Debating Talks with Iran on Nuclear Issue," *New York Times*, May 27, 2006, p. 1.

102. Condoleezza Rice, *No Higher Honor* (New York: Random House, 2011), 464.

103. IAEA Report, "Islamic Republic of Iran's Response to the Package Presented on June 6, 2006," Institute for Science and International Security, September 11, 2006, accessed November 20, 2012, http://isis-online.org/publications/iran/responsetext.pdf. See Arms Control Association, "History of Official Proposals," summary, 3.

104. Kenneth Katzman, *Iran: U.S. Concerns and Policy Responses*, CRS, CRS Report RL32048, November 1, 2006, 19, accessed November 20, 2012, http://fpc.state.gov/documents/organization/76319.pdf.

105. Elaine Sciolino, "Iran's Proposal to End Nuclear Standoff is Rejected by the West," *New York Times*, October 4, 2006, A6.

106. Sheryl Gay Stolberg and Kate Zernike, "Bush Backs Away From 2 Key Ideas of Panel on Iraq," *New York Times,* December 8, 2006, A1, accessed November 20, 2012.

107. "Security Council Imposes Sanctions on Iran For Failure to Halt Uranium Enrichment, Unanimously Adopting Resolution 1737 (2006)," Security Council 5612th Meeting, accessed November 17, 2012, http://www.un.org/News/Press/docs/2006/sc8928.doc.htm.

108. Sheryl Gay Stolberg, "Cheney, Like President, Has a Warning for Iran," *New York Times,* October 22, 2007, A8.

109. Tim Shipman and Colin Freeman, "Iran rejects Barack Obama's hand of friendship," *The Telegraph,* March 21, 2009, accessed January 11, 2013, http://www.telegraph.co.uk/news/worldnews/middleeast/iran/5026873/Iran-rejects-Barack-Obamas-hand-of-friendship.html.

110. AFP, "Obama Urges Iranians to End Decades of Animosity," *Daily Star* (Bangladesh), March 21, 2009, accessed November 17, 2009, http://thedailystar.net/newDesign/news-details.php?nid=80637.

111. Iason Athanasiadis, "Obama Sent Second Letter to Khamenei," *Washington Times,* September 3, 2009, accessed January 11, 2013, http://www.washingtontimes.com/news/2009/sep/03/obama-sent-second-letter-to-irans-khamenei/?page=all.

112. Shipman and Freeman, "Iran Rejects."

113. Julian Borger, "Iran agrees to send uranium abroad after talks breakthrough," *The Guardian,* October 1, 2009, accessed November 17, 2012, http://www.guardian.co.uk/world/2009/oct/01/iran-uranium-enrichment-plant-inspection.

114. Trita Parsi, *A Single Roll of the Dice: Obama's Diplomacy with Iran* (New Haven, CT: Yale University Press, 2012), 147–50.

115. Comprehensive Iran Sanctions, Accountability, and Divestment Act of 2010 H.R. 2194, 111th Cong. (2010), accessed November 20, 2012, http://www.gpo.gov/fdsys/pkg/BILLS-111hr2194enr/pdf/BILLS-111hr21 94enr.pdf.

116. Briefing on New Rewards for Justice Reward Offer, U.S. Department of State, December 22, 2011, accessed November 20, 2012, http://www.state.gov/r/pa/prs/ps/2011/12/179654.htm.

117. Adam Entous, "Panetta Pushes Iraq on Attacks," *Wall Street Journal,* July 11, 2011, accessed November 20, 2012, http://online.wsj.com/article/SB10001424052702304584404576437841398881406.html.

118. Office of Public Affairs, press release," Two Men Charged in Alleged Plot to Assassinate Saudi Arabian Ambassador to the United States," US Department of Justice, October 11, 2011, accessed November

20, 2012, http://www.justice.gov/opa/pr/2011/October/11-ag-1339
.html.

119. Anne Bayefsky, "Obama's Iran Policy: A Timeline," *National Review Online*, October 8, 2012, accessed November 20, 2012, http://www.nationalreview.com/corner/329718/obama-s-iran-policy-time line-anne-bayefsky. From 2009 on, Obama Administration officials have repeatedly warned Iran that the window for meaningful engagement would not remain open indefinitely, but such statements have proved insufficient to convince Iran to take advantage of the invitation to engage.

Chapter Four

1. Lowe, "Iran"; see note 45 in Chapter One, pp. 23–4 of source cited. Lowe calls a preventive attack "illegal warfare"and notes former UN inspector Hans Blix's critique of the lack of sufficient evidence to justify the US attack on Iraq. Peter Berkowitz, in "Would a Military Strike Against Iran be Legal?," *Real Clear Politics*, March 2, 2012, accessed November 20, 2012, http://www.realclearpolitics.com/articles/2012/03/02/would_a_military_strike_against_iran_be_legal.html, argues for the more flexible meaning of "imminence" adopted by the George W. Bush administration, and concludes that the law would side with an attack on Iran's nuclear facilities; his argument appears to assume, however, that Iran would, at the time of an attack, be "nuclear-armed." Robbie Sabel, former Legal Advisor to Israel's Foreign Ministry, describes the issues involved in determining the legality of a preventive strike on Iran's nuclear programs, but he makes no assertion that such a strike, particularly by the US, would be lawful. Robbie Sabel, "The Legality of an Attack on Iranian Nuclear Facilities," The Institute for National Security Studies, Insight No. 345, June 15, 2012, accessed January 12, 2013, http://www.inss.org.il/research.php?cat=3&incat=& read=6732.

2. Amitai Etzioni, in "Can a Nuclear-Armed Iran Be Deterred?" *Military Review* (May-June 2010): 117, 124, writes that objections to attacking Iran's nuclear sites point to the option of compelling "the regime to change its behavior by causing ever-higher levels of 'pain.'" Schake, in *Dealing with a Nuclear Iran*, 21, suggests a possible "demonstration strike" against targets unmistakably connected to the nuclear program to show Iran's vulnerability to attack.

3. *Laws of Armed Conflict v. Human Rights: International Humanitarian Law*, Part II: Art 25: Persons Interned in Neutral Territory, International

Committee of the Red Cross, 15, accessed November 21, 2012, http://www.hornstrand.net/kandidatuppsatser/LOAC_vs_HRL _APPENDIX_5.pdf.

4. The ICJ has in some contexts restricted the right of self-defense to attacks attributable to a state. See the court's decision rejecting Uganda's position that it could use force in self-defense against irregular forces attacking its territory from the Congo and could occupy parts of that country. See *Democratic Republic of Congo v. Uganda*, "Case Concerning Armed Activities on the Territory of Congo: Reports of Judgments, Advisory Opinions and Orders," International Court of Justice, December 19, 2005, accessed January 12, 2013, www.icj-cij.org/docket/files/ 116/10455.pdf. In *"Legal Consequences of the Construction of a Wall in the Occupied Palestinian Territory,"* International Court of Justice, July 9, 2004, 182, accessed November 21, 2012, http://www.icj-cij.org/docket/ files/131/1671.pdf, the ICJ rejected Israel's claim that the right of self-defense against terrorists in the occupied territories allowed it to build a fence within those territories. Compare the more sensible and convincing treatment by Daniel Bethlehem, "Self-Defense Against an Imminent or Actual Armed Attack by Nonstate Actors," *American Journal of International Law*, October 2012, 769.

5. An excellent source on these issues is Tal Becker's *Terrorism and the State: Rethinking the Rules of State Responsibility* (Portland, OR: Hart Publishing, 2006), 329–30.

6. President Reagan, "Transcript: The President's News Conference," January 7, 1986, The American Presidency Project, accessed November 21, 2012, http://www.presidency.ucsb.edu/ws/index.php ?pid=36812#axzz1niVcL2eH.

7. For a useful description of these risks, see Nathan Hodge, "In War Against Iran, U.S. Firepower Would Vie With Guerrilla Tactics," *Wall Street Journal*, April 14, 2012, accessed November 21, 2012, http:// online.wsj.com/article/SB100014240527023041771045773144440 82569820.html.

8. Adam Entous and Julian E. Barnes, "U.S. Bulks Up Iran Defenses," *Wall Street Journal*, February 25–26, 2012, 1; Editorial, "Iran's Hormuz Threat," *Wall Street Journal*, December 29, 2011, A14 ("The Hormuz threat is another opportunity to set boundaries on Iran's rogue behavior.").

9. For a description of harassment in the 2003 period, see David B. Crist, "Iran's Small Boats Are a Big Problem," *New York Times*, January 20, 2008, 12, noting that "For 20 years, Tehran has been harassing us in the Persian Gulf."

10. The US Supreme Court in 1825 rejected the proposition that every ship "may appropriate so much of the ocean as she may deem necessary for her protection, and prevent any nearer approach"; the court also ruled that ships in international waters are "not at liberty to inflict injuries upon other innocent parties, simply because of conjectural dangers." *The Marianna Flora,* 24 U.S. 1, 43 (1825), accessed January 12, 2013, http://caselaw.lp.findlaw.com/scripts/getcase.pl?navby =case&court=us&vol=24&invol=1.

11. U.S. Navy, *The US Commander's Handbook on the Law of Naval Operations,* NWP 1–14M, Para. 2.5.3.1, pp. 2-6 to 2-7 (July 2007 edition). The International Maritime Organization's measures are contained in the Convention on the International Regulations for Preventing Collisions at Sea, 1972 (COLREGS), International Maritime Organization, October 20, 1972 (entered into force July 15, 1977), accessed January 12, 2013, http:// www.imo.org/about/conventions/listofconventions/pages/colreg .aspx.

12. COLREGS, Ibid. This is most generally reflected in Rule 2 of the regulations, which essentially mandate safety above all regardless of rules that suggest other priorities:

2. Responsibility
(a) Nothing in these Rules shall exonerate any vessel, or the owner, master or crew thereof, from the consequences of any neglect to comply with these Rules or of the neglect of any precaution which may be required by the ordinary practice of seamen, or by the special circumstances of the case.
(b) In construing and complying with these Rules due regard shall be had to all dangers of navigation and collision and to any special circumstances, including the limitations of the vessels involved, which may make a departure from these Rules necessary to avoid immediate danger.

13. Chairman, Joint Chiefs of Staff Instruction 3121.01 (1 Oct 94), "Standing Rules of Engagement for US Forces," October 1, 1994, Enclosure A, Para. 2, Policy, (b)(1)-(4).

14. *The Marianna Flora,* 43.

15. *The US Commander's Handbook,* Para. 1, Purpose and Scope, (a).

16. These criteria are identified and discussed in the Stanford Study on Preventive Force, published as Abraham D. Sofaer, *The Best Defense? Legitimacy & Preventive Force* (Stanford, CA: Hoover Press, 2010), 103–26.

17. At their 2012 meeting in Tehran, for example, the 120-nation Non-aligned Movement voted unanimously to support Iran's right to a

nuclear energy program. Thomas Erdbrink, *New York Times*, September 1, 2012, A4.

18. Lowe, "Iran," 24.

19. Crist, "Iran's Small Boats," 12.

20. General Martin Dempsey, interview, "Face the Nation, Transcript," *CBS News*, January 8, 2012, accessed January 12, 2013, http://www.cbsnews.com/8301-3460_162-57354647/face-the-nation-transcript-january-8-2012; Charles Robb and Charles Wald, et al., "Establishing a Credible Threat Against Iran's Nuclear Program," Bipartisan Policy Center (March 2012), accessed January 12, 2013, http://bipartisanpolicy.org/sites/default/files/Credible%20Military%20Option.pdf.

21. Lolita Baldor and Rebecca Santana, "U.S. Troops Must have Legal Immunity to Stay in Iraq," *The Seattle Times*, August 1, 2011, accessed November 21, 2012, http://seattletimes.nwsource.com/html/nationworld/2015788407_apmlusiraqmullen.html.

22. Eli Lake, "Israel's Secret Attack Plan: Electronic Warfare," *The Daily Beast*, November 16, 2011, accessed January 12, 2013, http://www.thedailybeast.com/articles/2011/11/16/israel-s-secret-iran-attack-plan-electronic-warfare.html.

23. E.g., Joshua Mitnick, Jay Solomon, and Gordon Fairclough, "Israel Says Iran Behind Deadly Blast in Europe," *Wall Street Journal*, July 19, 2012, A1 (referring to bombing of bus carrying Israeli tourists in Bulgaria). Attacks have also taken place on Israeli diplomats in several countries. After cyber attacks on Saudi Aramco and US banks in various locations, Secretary of Defense Panetta said the US "was facing the possibility of a 'cyber-Pearl Harbor'. . . ." Elisabeth Bumiller and Thom Shanker, "Panetta Warns of Dire Threat of Cyber Attack on US," *New York Times*, October 12, 2012, A6; Thom Shanker and David E. Sanger, "Iran's Hand is Suspected in Computer Attacks," *New York Times*, October 14, 2012, A11; Siobhan Gorman, "Iran Renews Internet Attacks on U.S. Banks," *Wall Street Journal*, October 18, 2012, A11.

24. Matthew Levitt, "Why Iran Wants to Attack the United States," *Foreign Policy*, October 29, 2012, http://www.foreignpolicy.com/articles/2012/10/29/why_iran_wants_to_attack_the_united_states?page-full.

25. Zbigniew Brzezinski and Robert M. Gates, *Iran: Time for a New Approach* (New York: Council on Foreign Relations, 2004). The report states that "Given the potential threat that Iran's acquisition of nuclear weapons could pose, the full range of alternatives—including military options—for confronting Tehran must be examined." However, the report actually examines only a preventive strike on Iran's nuclear sys-

tem, noting all the dangers and the risk of failure. It does not look into the possible consequences of limited strikes in response to IRGC aggression. Jim Dobbins' RAND report is the most comprehensive of all the reports that deal with the Iranian threat, covering many related issues. With regard to the possible use of force, the report considers a preventive attack and its consequences, and it makes the general point that the US has the full range of uses of force available. At no point, however, does it attempt to address the possible use of force in self-defense, and its consequences. The use of force in self-defense would differ from "unprovoked" uses, which the report accurately points out are likely to provoke outrage and sympathy. Ibid., 111. The same failure to examine the utility of limited force in self-defense is true of the Iran Project Report, discussed in the text.

26. An exception is Elliot Abrams, who calls for a "new policy: that neither Iran nor any other government can kill Americans with impunity," in "What Happens When Iran Kills American Soldiers?" *Council on Forieign Relations Blog*, July 8, 2011, accessed November 21, 2012, http://blogs.cfr.org/abrams/2011/07/08/what-happens-when -Iran-kills-american-soldiers/.

27. Helene Cooper, "Sanctions Against Iran Grow Tighter, but What's the Next Step?," *New York Times*, January 24, 2012, accessed January 14, 2013, http://www.nytimes.com/2012/01/25/world/middle east/iran-sanctions-grow-tighter-but-whats-next.html. According to Cooper, many experts believe that "sanctions are their only real option, not because they necessarily believe that they will work, but because the other alternatives—a military strike, or doing nothing as Iran acquires a weapon—are unacceptable." She quotes R. Nicholas Burns, former Undersecretary of State under George W. Bush, as stating: "If there were an alternative to the sanctions, that would be one thing, . . . But is there? No.").

28. "Iran: If Israel Attacks Us, We'll Hit its Nuclear Sites," *Haaretz*, July 25, 2009, accessed November 21, 2012, http://www.haaretz.com/ news/iran-if-israel-attacks-us-we-ll-hit-its-nuclear-sites-1.280702.

29. On December 27, 2011, Iran's First Vice President, Mohammad Reza Rahimi, warned that if the West "impose sanctions on Iran's oil exports, then not even one drop of oil can flow through the Strait of Hormuz." David E. Sanger and Annie Lowrey, "Iran Threatens to Block Oil Shipments, as U.S. Prepares Sanctions," *New York Times*, December 27, 2011, accessed January 14, 2013, http://www.nytimes.com/2011/ 12/28/world/middleeast/iran-threatens-to-block-oil-route-if -embargo-is-imposed.html?pagewanted=all.

30. John Frisby, "Iran's Hormuz Threat"; see Chapter Four note 8 above.

31. Michael Petrou, "Iran is Turning into a Military Dictatorship," in *Iran: Current Controversies*, ed. Debra A. Miller (Farmington Hills, MI: Greenhaven Press, 2011), 140.

32. Geoffrey Kemp, "The Reagan Administration," in *The Iran Primer*, digital book, United States Institute of Peace, Washington, DC, accessed November 21, 2012, http://iranprimer.usip.org/resource/reagan-administration.

33. David F. Winkler, "Operation Praying Mantis Blows a Hole in Iranian Navy," *No Higher Honor*, Navy League of the United States, September 2003, accessed November 21, 2012, http://www.navyleague.org/sea_power/sep_03_45.php.

34. Norman Podhoretz, "World War IV: How It Started, What It Means, and Why We Have to Win," *Commentary* (September 2004), accessed November 21, 2012, http://www.commentarymagazine.com/article/world-war-iv-how-it-started-what-it-means-and-why-we-have-to-win/. Bin Laden stated in a 1998 interview with John Miller, for example, that Al Qaeda soldiers "were surprised at the low morale of the American soldiers and realized, more than before, that the American soldier was a paper tiger and after a few blows ran in defeat."

35. Final Report of the National Commission on Terrorist Attacks upon the United States, 9/11 Commission, released July 26, 2004, 1–26, accessed January 14, 2013, www.9-11commission.gov/report/911Report.pdf.

36. Tony Capaccio and John Walcott, "Iran Stepping Up Spying, Support for Terror, Clapper Says," *Bloomberg News*, January 31, 2012, accessed January 14, 2013, http://www.bloomberg.com/news/2012-01-31/iran-stepping-up-spying-support-for-terror.html.

37. Richard Clarke and Steven Simon, "Bombs That Would Backfire," *New York Times*, April 16, 2006, 13, accessed January 14, 2013, http://www.nytimes.com/2006/04/16/opinion/16clarke.html. While the authors write that "there is a role for threats of force to back up diplomacy and help concentrate the minds of our allies," they claim that a "chilling threat" by the Clinton Administration after the Khobar Towers bombing "immobilized Iran's intelligence service. Iranian terrorism against the United States ceased."

38. Gold, *The Rise*, 23; Kissinger, in "A Nuclear Test," 109, writes, "any strategy must count on a somewhat rational enemy; nothing can deter an opponent bent on self-destruction."

39. In April 1980, for example, five months after Iran seized the US embassy and staff in Tehran, the United States was able to secure

support from European allies for even relatively weak sanctions only after it threatened to start mining Iran's harbors. Pollack, *The Persian Puzzle*, 167–70.

40. Alexander Marquardt, "U.S. Denies Role in Iranian Nuclear Scientist's Assassination," *ABC News*, January 11, 2012, accessed November 21, 2012, http://abcnews.go.com/Blotter/iranian-nuclear-scientist -killed-amid-heightened-tensions/story?id=15338086#.T0K06hzabHw.

41. Ibid.

42. Amir Taheri, "The Problem With Talking to Iran," *Wall Street Journal*, May 28, 2008, A17. The author says, "Mr. Ahmadinejad is talking about changing the destiny of mankind, while Mr. Obama and his foreign policy experts offer spare parts for Boeings or membership in the World Trade Organization."

43. Michael Slackman and Nazila Fathi, "On Two Fronts, One Nuclear, Iran is Defiant," *Herald Tribune*, September 3, 2007, accessed January 14, 2013, http://www.heraldtribune.com/article/20070903/ ZNYT03/709030682; Jay Solomon, "Iran Touts Nuke Gain Ahead of U.S. Talks," *Wall Street Journal*, December 6, 2010, A1; David E. Sanger, "Iran Trumpets Nuclear Ability At a Second Location," *New York Times*, January 9, 2012, A1; Jay Solomon, "Tehran is Ramping Up Nuclear-Fuel Output," *Wall Street Journal*, February 25–26, 2012, A8.

44. General Martin Dempsey, interview by Barbara Starr, "Top General Says Iran Shouldn't 'Miscalculate Our Resolve'," *CNN*, December 21, 2011, accessed November 21, 2012, http://edition.cnn.com/2011/12/ 20/us/top-general-iran/index.html.

Chapter Five

1. George P. Shultz, "Foreword," in *Reagan: A Life in Letters*, eds. Kiron K. Skinner, Annelise Anderson, and Martin Anderson (New York: Free Press, 2004).

2. "The American Experience: Reagan," PBS, executive producer Austin Hoyt (Los Angeles, CA: WGBH Educational Foundation, 1998), transcript, accessed January 14, 2013, http://www.pbs.org/wgbh/ americanexperience/features/transcript/reagan-transcript/.

3. US Department of State, Memorandum of Conversation (MOC), Reagan-Gorbachev, Third Meeting, 10:00 am-1:35 pm, October 12, 1986, p. 18, accessed January 14, 2013, http://www.gwu.edu/~nsarchiv/ NSAEBB/NSAEBB203/index.html.

4. "Shultz, Shevardnadze Step Up Effort To Resolve Daniloff Case," *New York Times*, September 26, 1986, accessed November 21, 2012, http://

articles.sun-sentinel.com/1986-09-26/news/8602260673_1_daniloff
-gerasimov-soviet-dissidents.

5. Mark Bowden, *Guests of the Ayatollah: The Iran Hostage Crisis: The First Battle in America's War with Militant Islam* (New York: Atlantic Monthly Press, 2006), 577.

6. Steven Erlanger, "Citing Options, Iran Rejects Uranium Deal, Diplomat Says," *New York Times,* January 24, 2011, accessed November 21, 2012, http://www.nytimes.com/2011/01/25/world/middleeast/25iran.html.

7. Tony Karon, "Iran's Geneva Offer on Nukes: Progress for All," *Time*, October 2, 2009, accessed November 21, 2012, http://www.time.com/time/world/article/0,8599,1927537,00.html.

8. President Barack Obama, "Remarks on the Natural Disasters in the South Pacific and Indonesia and the Situation in Iran," October 1, 2009, http://www.gpo.gov/fdsys/pkg/DCPD-200900769/content-detail.html. President Obama commented: "Iran must demonstrate its commitment to transparency. Earlier this month, we presented clear evidence that Iran has been building a covert nuclear facility in Qom. Since Iran has now agreed to cooperate fully and immediately with the International Atomic Energy Agency, it must grant unfettered access to IAEA inspectors within 2 weeks." He went on to say, "We're committed to serious and meaningful engagement. But we're not interested in talking for the sake of talking. If Iran does not take steps in the near future to live up to its obligations, then the United States will not continue to negotiate indefinitely, and we are prepared to move towards increased pressure."

9. "Mousavi Slams Govt Policy in Geneva Talks," *Frontline*, October 29, 2009, accessed November 21, 2012, http://www.pbs.org/wgbh/pages/frontline/tehranbureau/2009/10/selected-headlines-57.html.

10. "History of Official Proposals on the Iranian Nuclear Issue," Arms Control Association, April 12, 2012, updated January 2013, accessed January 14, 2013, http://www.armscontrol.org/factsheets/Iran_Nuclear_Proposals.

11. US Department of State, Memorandum Of Conversation, Reagan-Gorbachev Meetings in Reykjavik, 10:40 am–12:30 pm, October 11, 1986, 4, http://www.gwu.edu/~nsarchiv/NSAEBB/NSAEBB203/Document09.pdf.

12. President Reagan, "Remarks at the Annual Convention of the National Association of Evangelicals in Orlando, Florida," March 8, 1983, http://www.reagan.utexas.edu/archives/speeches/1983/30883b.htm.

13. US Department of State, Memorandum of Conversation, Reagan-Gorbachev Meetings in Reykjavik, 10:00 am–1:35 pm, October 12,

1986, 15, accessed January 14, 2013, http://www.gwu.edu/~nsarchiv/ NSAEBB/NSAEBB203/Document13.pdf.

14. George P. Shultz, *Ideas and Action: Featuring the 10 Commandments of Negotiating* (Erie, PA: Free to Choose Press, 2010), 89.

15. James Risen, "Gingrich Wants Funds for Covert Action in Iran," *Los Angeles Times*, December 10, 1995, accessed November 21, 2012, http://articles.latimes.com/1995-12-10/news/mn-12511_1_covert -action.

16. *Argentine Republic v. Ameranda Hess Shipping Corp.*, 488 U.S. 428 (1989), accessed January 14, 2013, http://supreme.justia.com/cases/ federal/us/488/428/case.html.

17. *Carl Marks & Co. v. U.S.S.R.*, 665 F. Supp. 323 (S.D. NY 1987), accessed November 21, 2012, http://inkom.com.au/sites/default/files/ Carl%20Marx%20vs%20USSR%2 0case%20full4 286932100395650.pdf.

18. See Declaration of Abraham D. Sofaer, *Guy Von Dardel v. Union of Soviet Socialist Republics*, Civil Action No. 84–035 (S.D.N.Y. 1989).

19. The Antiterrorism and Effective Death Penalty Act of 1996, Pub. L. No. 104–132, 110 Stat. 1214 (1996), accessed January 14, 2013, http:// www.uscis.gov/ilink/docView/PUBLAW/HTML/PUBLAW/ 0-0-0-8598. html; Matthew J. Peed, "Blacklisting as Foreign Policy: The Politics and Law of Listing Terror States," *Duke Law Journal* 54 (2005): 1321–54; Note on the Foreign Sovereign Immunities Act, in Steven N. Avruch, "The 1983 Korean Air Lines Incident: Highlighting the Law of International Air Carrier Liability," *Boston College International and Comparative Law Review* 8, no. 1 (1985), 76–126.

20. Jennifer K. Elsea, *Suits Against Terrorist States by Victims of Terrorism*, Congressional Research Service Report for Congress, RL31258, August 8, 2008, accessed January 14, 2013, www.fas.org/sgp/crs/ terror/RL31258.pdf.

21. Katzman, *Iran Sanctions*; see Chapter One note 37 above, p. 36 of source cited.

22. Article 45, Vienna Convention on Diplomatic Relations, 23 U.S.T. 3227, April 18, 1961, 500 U.N.T.S. 95; Sean Vitrano, "Hell-Bent On Awarding Recovery to Terrorism Victims: The Evolution and Application of the Antiterrorism Amendments to the Foreign Sovereign Immunities Act," *Dickinson Journal of International Law* 19 (2000), 213–44.

23. *Victims of Trafficking and Violence Protection Act of 2000*, Public L. No. 106–386, 114 STAT. 1464, Sec. 2002, October 28, 2000, accessed November 21, 2012, http://www.state.gov/documents/organization/10492.pdf.

24. *Flatow v. Islamic Republic of Iran*, 76 F. Supp. 2d 16, 19 n.3 (DC 1999); see Katzman, *Iran Sanctions*, Chapter One note 37 above, p. 36,

pointing out that Congress was considering legislation that would have made funds held by a clearing organization subject to execution to satisfy judgments against Iran for terrorist acts.

25. Steven R. Weisman, "U.S. is Debating Talks with Iran on Nuclear Issue," *New York Times*, May 27, 2006, 1, quoting Richard L. Armitage, former Deputy Secretary of State, after he had left the Bush administration: "Some people in the administration think that diplomacy is a sign of weakness. In fact, it can show you're strong."

26. Kissinger, "A Nuclear Test," A17.

27. Shultz, *Turmoil and Triumph*, 278.

28. *Islamic Republic of Iran v. United States of America* (concerning oil platforms), Summary of the Judgment of 6 November 2003, International Court of Justice, accessed January 14, 2013, http://www.icj-cij .org/docket/?sum=634&code=op&p1=3&p2=3&case=90&k=0a&p3=5.

29. Nick B. Williams Jr., "Iran Offers Help in Hostage Crisis: Rafsanjani Says U.S. Must Sway Israel and Avoid Military Moves," *Los Angeles Times*, August 5, 1989, accessed November 20, 2012, http://articles .latimes.com/1989–08–05/news/mn-437_1_hostage-crisis.

30. Address by George H.W. Bush, January 20, 1989, accessed January 14, 2013, http://www.inaugural.senate.gov/swearing-in/address/ address-by-george-h-w-bush-1989.

31. "Iran Charged over Argentina Bomb" *BBC News*, October 25, 2006, accessed November 21, 2012, http://news.bbc.co.uk/2/hi/6085 768.stm.

32. Giandomenico Picco, *Man Without a Gun: One Diplomat's Secret Struggle to Free the Hostages, Fight Terrorism, and End a War* (New York: Times Books, 1999), 4–5, wrote, "My failure to deliver the American side of the deal with the Iranians essentially rendered me a liar, and I had to face up to the fact that if I were to have any chance to reclaim my integrity, one more trip would be required. I could hardly expect the United Nations' new secretary-general, Boutros Boutros-Gali, to understand or to pop for a ticket to Teheran. But this was personal now: going to Tehran was exactly what I had to do. I had to look into the eyes of President Ali Akbar Hashemi Rafsanjani and acknowledge my inadvertent deception."

33. Pollack, *The Persian Puzzle*, 252.

34. James Dobbins, *Negotiating with Iran* (Santa Monica, CA: RAND Corporation, 2007), accessed November 20, 2012, http://www.rand. org/content/dam/rand/pubs/testimonies/2007/RAND\eCT293.pdf.

35. James Dobbins, "Negotiating with Iran: Lessons from Personal Experience," *The Washington Quarterly* 33, no. 1 (January 2010), 157. For

Rumsfeld's thoughts on negotiating during this period, see Donald Rumsfeld, *Known and Unknown: A Memoir* (New York: Penguin Group, 2011), 636–9.

36. Katzman, *Iran Sanctions*; see Chapter One note 37, p. 35 of source cited. Iran's interest in obtaining satisfaction for its claims is widely underestimated. The military claims yet to be decided seek many billions of dollars, and the CRS estimates the value of property frozen in recent years to be $48 billion.

37. Mehdi Khalaji, "Iran and the Human Rights Opening," *Wall Street Journal*, August 8, 2012, A15; Lowe, *Iran*, 25, notes, "For [human rights lawyer Shirin] Ebadi, any nuclear talks must act as a stepping stone to address more urgent issues, such as civil and political rights."

38. Flyntt Leverett and Hillary Mann, "What We Wanted to Tell You About Iran," *New York Times*, December 22, 2006, A31. Leverett and Mann have advocated full-fledged engagement with Iran. They attribute the opposition to their views to the desire for "regime change." They do not address the possible use of limited force in self-defense as a means of applying pressure to bring Iran to the table and to give the US president who attempts to negotiate credibility with Congress.

39. Documentary film, "The Cold War: Geneva: The Giants Meet," *Turmoil and Triumph: The George Shultz Years*, DVD, directed by David deVries (Los Angeles: Free to Choose Media, 2010) accessed November 20, 2012, http://www.turmoilandtriumph.org/coldwar/geneva_summit.php.

40. Thomas Erdbrink, "Iran Denies Plan to End Nuclear Standoff," *New York Times*, October 6, 2012, accessed November 20, 2012, http://www.nytimes.com/2012/10/07/world/middleeast/iran-denies-report-of-plan-to-end-nuclear-standoff.html. Iran reportedly proposed a nine-step plan at the P5+1 negotiations in July 2012, said to contain several positive elements (including a total cessation of enrichment at levels higher than required for power generation), but demanded disproportionately significant concessions in exchange. US officials felt obliged to dismiss the plan publicly as "unworkable." This led Iranian officials to deny ever having presented such a plan.

41. In addition to the games played by the arms dealers in the Iran/Contra Affair, a particularly embarrassing incident took place when the Ayatollah Khomeini publicly released a letter purportedly from President Carter but actually forged by Hector Villalon, an Argentine businessman used by the Carter Administration as an interlocutor, accepting guilt for numerous "injustices." Villalon forged the document in the desperate hope that it would convince Khomeini to open

negotiations with the United States on the hostages. Pollack, *The Persian Puzzle*, 165.

Conclusion

1. Henry A. Kissinger, *Nuclear Weapons and Foreign Policy* (New York: W. W. Norton & Company, 1969—abridged edition), 57.

2. Chester A. Crocker, "The Art of Peace: Bringing Diplomacy Back to Washington," *Foreign Affairs* 86, no. 4 (July/August 2007), accessed November 20, 2012, http://www.foreignaffairs.com/print/62670.

3. Gold, *The Rise*, 185–9, cites the doctrine of *taqiya*, or showing a false intention, as well as an Iranian proverb: "A lie which brings benefit is preferable to a truth which causes damage." He concludes: "Iranians and the West were simply playing the diplomatic game by very different sets of rules." Such doctrines and proverbs are of course common to many cultures, and relying on the "word" of diplomats would be foolhardy regardless of the states involved.

About the Author

braham D. Sofaer is the George P. Shultz Distinguished Scholar and Senior Fellow at Stanford University's Hoover Institution. He graduated from the New York University School of Law in 1965, where he was editor in chief of the Law Review. He clerked for Judge J. Skelly Wright of the US Court of Appeals for the DC Circuit and for US Supreme Court Justice William J. Brennan, Jr. Sofaer served as an assistant US attorney in the Southern District of New York from 1967 to 1969, under Robert J. Morgenthau, Jr., after which he was a professor of law at the Columbia University School of Law until 1979. That year, he was appointed to the federal district court in the Southern District of New York, where he served until 1985, when he became legal adviser to the US Department of State.

During his tenure as legal adviser, Sofaer served as agent for the United States to The Hague Tribunal on US/Iranian claims. In that capacity he supervised the submission of briefs, argued some cases, and led a successful effort to speed up the disposition of claims through settlements, working directly with Iranian officials. He also led the successful settlement negotiations for the US in other significant matters, including the dispute between Egypt and Israel over the final border at Taba; the recovery from Iraq of claims for US navy personnel aboard the USS *Stark*; sovereign-immunity and extradition-treaty negotiations with several nations, including the Soviet Union; the compensation claim for the Letelier assassination; the claims by US and Israeli victims stemming from the killings at Ras Burqa; and negotiation of the Maritime Terrorism Convention. He received the Distinguished Service Award in 1989 for service to the Department of State as a non-civil servant.

In 2010, Sofaer published *The Best Defense? Legitimacy and Preventive Force*, the report of the Stanford Study Group on Preventive Force chaired by former Secretary of State George P. Shultz and Dr. Coit Blacker, director of the Freeman Spogli Institute for Foreign Affairs. Further information on Sofaer's background and activities can be found at www.hoover.org/fellows/10685 and at www.abesofaer.com.

Index